ANTINORI

DOMAINE LEFLAIVE

R. LÓPEZ DE HEREDIA

GAJA

JOH. JOS. PRÜM

ROMANÉE-CONTI

DOMAINE DE LA
ROMANÉE-CONTI

GAJA

VIÑA
TONDONIA

E. GUIGAL

CATENA ZAPATA

CHÂTEAU D'YQUEM

HENSCHKE

CÔTE RÔTIE

CHÂTEAU
LAFITE ROTHSCHILD

HENSCHKE

HARLAN ESTATE

ANTINORI

DOMAINE LEFLAIVE

EREDIA

D1520493

ROMANÉE-CONTI

DOMAINE DE LA
ROMANÉE-CONTI

GAJA

GAJA

VIÑA
TONDONIA

JOH. JOS. PRÜM

E. GUIGAL

CATENA ZAPATA

CHÂTEAU D'YQUEM

CÔTE RÔTIE

CHÂTEAU
LAFITE ROTHSCHILD

HENSCHKE

HARLAN ESTATE

GOLD
in the
vineyards

GOLD
in the
vineyards

ILLUSTRATED STORIES OF THE WORLD'S
MOST CELEBRATED VINEYARDS

Laura Catena

Catapulta

★ INDEX ★

Introduction
The ripening of vineyard gold
6

Château Lafite Rothschild
The first of firsts
11

Solaia
**The oldest family
winery in the world**
25

Château d'Yquem
The noble rot
39

Viña Tondonia
Tradition above all
53

Harlan Estate
**The California
adventurer**
67

Romanée-Conti
**A world
heritage wine**
81

Wehlener Sonnenuhr
A German clock
95

Leflaive Montrachet
The queen of wines
109

Hill of Grace
**The Old World
in Australia**
123

Sorì San Lorenzo
**The Holy Grail
of Piedmont**
139

La Mouline
**Red and white
make magic**
151

Adrianna Vineyard
**The *Grand Cru*
of South America**
165

Biography
Laura Catena
181

The Ripening of Vineyard Gold

My Italian *nonno* called me La Lauchita (the little mouse) because I couldn't stop moving. And that is why my great-grandmother Nicasia, who rarely ever disobeyed my mother, was willing to let me play during the *siesta* nap hour. I still treasure the dress Nicasia knit for Dolly, a blonde doll with pink cheeks that my parents had bought for me in Buenos Aires, and who accompanied me on those quiet Mendoza afternoons.

This book, *Gold in the Vineyards*, began to take shape in Argentina, during my childhood, when Nicasia taught me that adults could and should play…and I haven't stopped since.

As a girl I was a tireless reader, although I admit to first checking out a book's drawings and photos because the desire to see illustrations consumed me. When I became a teenager and the illustrations disappeared in my adult books, it was a big disappointment. That is why, when I had my own children, I was overjoyed to be able once again to skip through the written pages and let the images tell the story. From there was born the inspiration to create an illustrated book like the ones I loved so much as a girl, this time about wine. Great wines, like classic books, have the characteristic of being unforgettable.

In the 1990s, I joined my father in his quest to make Argentine wines that could stand with the best in the world. From that point on, my life would be split between practicing medicine and making Argentine wine. At that time Argentine wine was very much under the radar —and our journey felt in many ways like that of *Don Quixote de la Mancha*, risky and uncertain. During those years I became a scholar of the great vineyards of the world and came to the realization that finding a special vineyard site is like searching for gold. Like gold-rush gold diggers, we winemakers are driven by zeal and passion, but ultimately our guiding stars are luck and destiny. When we come upon a magical vineyard site, it's like finding undiscovered gold.

The chapters of this book are made up of the passions, personalities, and special pebbles of vineyards that have blessed a family with their gold. I invite you to dream, to skip to the end of this book through its illustrations, and to enjoy, with a glass of wine at hand, the small heroisms of the history of wine and its vineyards.

Laura Catena

To the women in my family:

To my great-grandmother Nicasia,
who taught me how to play and love.

To my grandmother Angélica,
who unfortunately I never met but
who, through my father, taught me
to admire the intelligence of women.

**To my maternal
grandmother, "La Acicita,"**
who encouraged me to write
poetry and seek adventure.

To my mother, Elena,
who (against my father's fears)
let me travel to Paris alone,
at the age of 14, to study
French and Art History.

To my sister Adrianna
(Doctor of History, a graduate of
Oxford University —I'm so proud!),
for teaching me that history is the sum
of millions of personal accounts.

To Nicola,
my daughter and tireless playmate.

**To my mother-in-law Nina,
my nieces, cousins, aunts
and sisters-in-law,**
who have given me so much love when
I, in my frenzied, quixotic journey,
do not reciprocate as I should.

PAUILLAC, BORDEAUX

CHÂTEAU LAFITE ROTHSCHILD

Château Lafite Rothschild
The first of firsts

The King's wine

"Youth is the period of possibility."
<u>Ambrose Bierce</u>

<u>Louis Pasteur</u> thought there was more wisdom in wine than in all the books in the world; and the **Maréchal de Richelieu** was fully convinced that wine held the secret to **eternal youth**.

Of course, not just any wine possessed such qualities. To the Maréchal de Richelieu, there was only one, and that was Château Lafite.

Richelieu had so many titles that, while his arrival was being announced to **Louis XV**, king of France and Navarre, <u>the monarch had time to study Richelieu's complexion</u>. Louis XV was surprised to find the 59-year-old deeply rejuvenated.

The Lafite elixir immediately became the **"official wine" of the court** of **Louis XV**, DISPLACING THE USUAL VINEYARDS OF BURGUNDY and Champagne. Such was Lafite's success that Madame de Pompadour served it at each of her evening salons.

Louis François-Armand de Vignerot du Plessis had many titles: Maréchal de Richelieu and Fronsac, Prince of Mortagne, Marquis de Pont-Courlay, Count of Cosnac, Baron de Cozes, Baron de Barbezieux, Baron de Saujon, Maréchal and Peer of France.

As for the Maréchal Richelieu, he may have been right about the eternal youth **hidden in every glass** of Château Lafite: After having fought innumerable duels and enjoyed amorous adventures throughout Europe, after showing commendable courage in bloody battles and facing imprisonment, Richelieu, Maréchal of France, maintained his **strength**, **lucidity** and **vigor** until the ripe age of 92.

The wine's name can be traced to the abbot **Gombaud de Lafite**, who in 1234 left a mark on the land so resonant that we speak of him and his vines almost a thousand years later.

In the **17th century** the winemaking reputation of the domaine **surged** in the hands of <u>Jacques de Ségur</u>, the man responsible for the vineyards we now know as Château Lafite.

London's aristocracy first recognized the quality of Lafite's wines and happily paid more for the Ségur wine than for the rest of the wines of Bordeaux.

The grandson of Jacques, <u>Nicolas Alexandre de Ségur</u>, inherited the vineyards of Lafite, and so great was his faith in the place that he doubled the surface of planted vines, upgraded the vineyard management and promoted his brand both abroad…and at the king's court!

Little wonder that Nicolas Alexandre developed a **reputation** as "prince of the vines" and his **rouge** became known as "the wine of kings."

Of the four wines classified as Premier Grand Cru Classés (in the official wine classification of Bordeaux of 1855), Lafite was considered by many to be the first of firsts.

On August 8, 1868, the history of Château Lafite would change forever. **Baron James de Rothschild**, from a renowned family of bankers, acquired the property and renamed the historic label "**CHÂTEAU LAFITE ROTHSCHILD**".

Twentieth-century hardships —including the first <u>World War</u> I and the financial crisis of the 1930s— **hit** the region so strongly that many vineyards were forced to reduce not only their costs but also the acreage of land under vine. As a result, the Rothschilds decided to concentrate their efforts on only 55 hectares of vineyards.

During <u>World War II</u>, all the properties of the Rothschilds were **confiscated** (as was the case for all those owned by Jewish families), and the Château was used as the base of communications for the Third Reich army.

In 1942, after enormous diplomatic efforts, the French government of Vichy managed to recover the property and put it in the hands of its heirs Alain and Elie Rothschild, who at that time were prisoners of war. Thanks to the Geneva Convention, their possessions were protected.

Baron James de Rothschild

"All refinement is cultural.
Both the pleasure of producing
fine wine and the pleasure of
building. And here, with this winery
and Ricardo Bofill, I have felt an
enormous amount of pleasure."

Baron Eric de Rothschild

Thus, many of the extremely valuable bottles stored away in the basement, some even from the 18th century, **survived** the war.

In 1974 **Eric de Rothschild** took the reins of Château Lafite Rothschild, infusing it with renewed energy and incorporating a vanguard technical team. Eric built the label's revolutionary **circular cava**, designed together with the Catalan architect Ricardo Bofill; it can hold up to 2,200 barrels.

A passionate lover of **art** and photography, Eric also invited renowned photographers such as Jacques Henri Lartigue, Irving Penn, Robert Doisneau and Richard Avedon to photograph the winery and vineyards, so that their images would be forever associated with his beloved Chateau Lafite Rothschild.

Elegance and balance

The plots, composed of <u>gravel</u> and <u>clay</u>, lie on a bed of <u>limestone</u> and have good exposure and excellent drainage.

One hundred and twelve hectares are cultivated with an average of 9,500 vines per hectare. About **16,000 cases** are produced at each harvest.

During the harvest, not all the grapes are extracted at their maximum level of maturity. What is sought is a balance between different levels of maturity. The objective is to obtain unique textures, a perceptible freshness and an aromatic character of incomparable complexity.

Aging: 18–20 months.

Type of barrel: 100% new French oak.

During the **harvest**, up to **450 PEOPLE** are hired to collect all the grapes in only ten days.

For Eric Kohler, technical director of Château Lafite Rothschild, the **human capital** is the key to the care of each vineyard and each plot, in addition to the precision of choosing the ideal moment for the harvest.

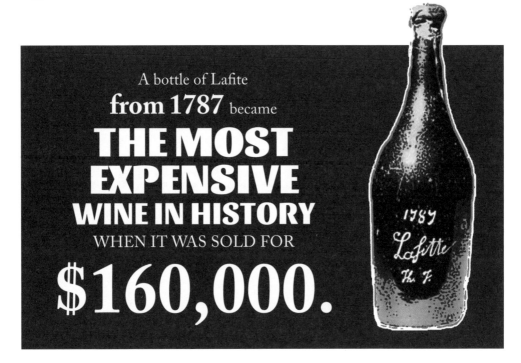

A bottle of Lafite
from 1787 became
THE MOST EXPENSIVE
WINE IN HISTORY
WHEN IT WAS SOLD FOR
$160,000.

The Château has been
IMMORTALIZED
through
images
by the most
prestigious
photographers
in the world,
including
RICHARD AVEDON.

Only **3**
FAMILIES
have OWNED
the Château since
the 17th century:
THE *Ségur* FAMILY,
THE
Vanlerberghe
FAMILY
AND THE
Rothschild
FAMILY.

ROBERT PARKER JR.,
the world's most influential
wine critic,
GAVE THE **PERFECT CLASSIFICATION**

OF **100**
POINTS
to the

1953

1982

1986

2003 2000 1996

vintages.

In the dialect of **Gascony,**

LAFITE *means*

"SMALL HILL"

FROM *TERROIR* TO BOTTLE

The vineyard is located in Pauillac, Bordeaux, France.

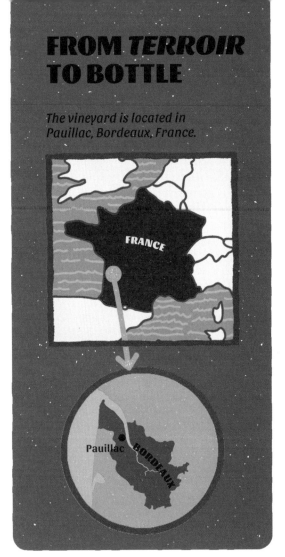

FRANCE

Pauillac BORDEAUX

The varieties of the blend

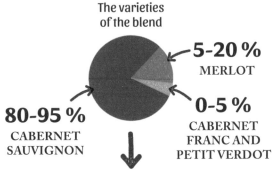

5-20 %
MERLOT

80-95 %
CABERNET SAUVIGNON

0-5 %
CABERNET FRANC AND PETIT VERDOT

Ancient vines

The average age of the vines is 39 years, although it should be noted that vines less than 10 years old are not included in the elaboration of the Grand Vin, which increases the average age of the vines that produce the Grand Vin to about 45 years.

{ The oldest plot, called La Gravière, was planted in 1886. }

The vineyard encompasses three main areas: the mounds surrounding the Château, the Carruades plateau immediately to the west and a plot of 4.5 hectares in the neighboring commune of Saint Estèphe.

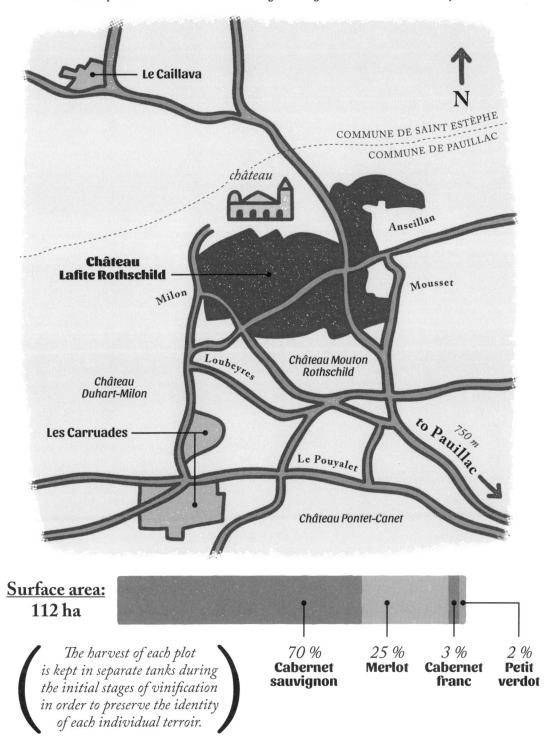

**Surface area:
112 ha**

The harvest of each plot is kept in separate tanks during the initial stages of vinification in order to preserve the identity of each individual terroir.

70 %
Cabernet sauvignon

25 %
Merlot

3 %
Cabernet franc

2 %
Petit verdot

Solaia

The oldest family winery in the world

Tuscan Passions

"It is wine that leads me on,
the wild wine that makes
the wisest man sing
at the top of his lungs,
and laugh like a fool
—it drives him to dance... it even
tempts him to blurt out stories
better never told."

The Odyssey, Homer

In Tuscany legend has it that **the origins** of the Antinori family, the most famous Italian wine producer in the world, **date back to Troy, more than a thousand years before the birth of Christ.** And that Antenor, who opposed the war with the Greek invaders, was a distinguished counselor at the Trojan court of King Priam.

The Roman poet Virgilio adds that Antenor survived the fall of the city by escaping to Italy, where he founded the city of Padua.

If this is true, then **Antenor** began, without even anticipating it, the saga of an extraordinary family, one that would be involved in wars, inventions, discoveries, passions, conquests, and producing centuries of delicate aromas and memorable flavors —and even a fair amount of big and small miracles. Or, as they call it in Europe, the Renaissance.

Documents confirm that by **1183**, Rinuccio di Antinoro was producing wine in **Castello di Combiate**, north of <u>Florence</u>. When the castle was besieged and destroyed soon thereafter, the family fled the fields and moved to the city. At that time, Florence was perhaps the most important cultural center in the world, and Antinori would become a member of **ARTE DELLA SETA**, the **SILK PRODUCERS'** organization that was key to the region's economy.

The Antinoris became **great entrepreneurs** through their involvement in **silk production, banking** and **politics**, never abandoning their principal trade: developing the land for **vineyards** and wine.

Some time later they joined the Society of Wine Producers of Florence, and soon their destiny was linked to that of the powerful Medici family.

Along with the discovery of America, **the Renaissance** would transform European reality forever. At that time the Antinori family produced 40 barrels of wine in Galluzzo, the property that the Antinoris owned to the south of the city, that was **APPRECIATED** by the great Florentine families. The Antinoris themselves were in charge of transporting and selling the wine.

In 1506, thanks to the **success** of the family businesses, Niccolo Antinori was able to acquire a **PALACE** next to the cathedral of Florence and in front of the church of San Giácomo.

Accariso Antinori would become a member of the silk producers' organization in Florence.

SETAS ANTINORI

The Antinori Palace

Bacco, *by the Italian Caravaggio, was painted around 1595.* The painting is currently in the Uffizi Gallery in Florence, Italy.

That building, known since then as the **Antinori Palace**, became the **heart** of the family businesses.

The **PRESTIGE** of the Antinori brand continued to grow. The poet Francesco Redi, personal wine critic for the Medicis, praised the Antinori wines in his poem ***Baco in Tuscany.*** However, it would not be the Antinori family's financial success that would end up leaving the most impact on Florence's nobility, but a story of a very different caliber.

In 1571, Piero de Medici, of the city's most important aristocratic family, married Leonor de Toledo, a beautiful girl of 18 who was kind, generous and loved by everyone who had the opportunity to meet her during her short life.

From a young age, Piero worried his parents by showing a **dark and cruel** spirit that persisted throughout his adult life despite the family's efforts to help him. Piero was irascible and terribly violent and wasted his fortune on gambling and women.

Leonor, devastated by the certainty of a nefarious future with her husband, approached Bernardino Antinori, a young hero of the battle of Lepanto, a member of the Order of St. Stephen and heir to the family famous for its vineyards.

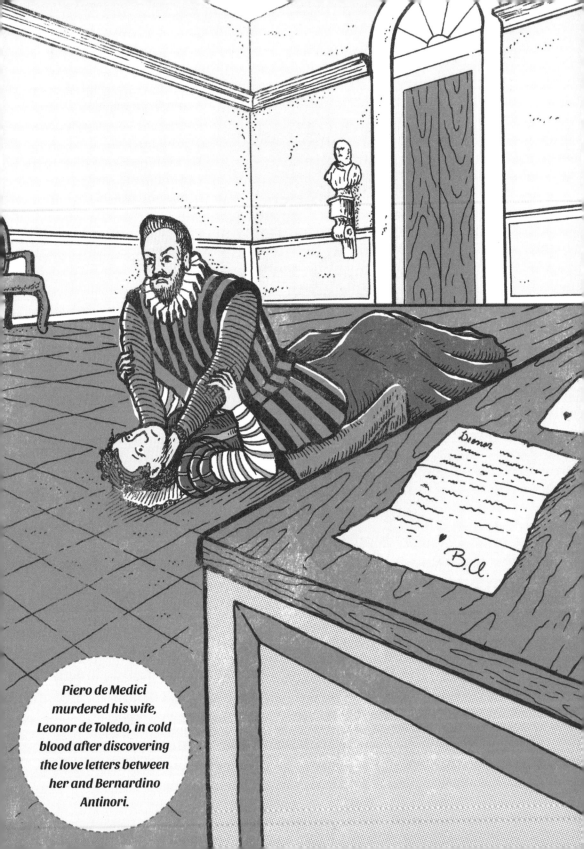

Piero de Medici murdered his wife, Leonor de Toledo, in cold blood after discovering the love letters between her and Bernardino Antinori.

"All my daughters have the two ingredients most necessary to produce wine: intelligence and passion."

Piero Antinori

After hearing rumors of the existence of this bond, Piero discovered **the love letters** and poignant poems written by Bernardino for Leonor. Piero de Medici did not hesitate to take his revenge. It was later revealed that while loudly accusing his wife of adultery, **PIERO MURDERED HER IN COLD BLOOD**, strangling her with a dog leash. Leonor was 23 years old. Bernardino Antinori was arrested shortly after, with no reason given for the arrest, and died mysteriously in his jail cell.

Two centuries later, wine-growing activity in Tuscany boomed as a result of interest abroad, especially in the United Kingdom; the Antinoris began to export their wines all over the world. In 1850, they acquired the Tignanello Vineyard, 47 hectares in Tuscany, to produce a wine that would quickly become a **world legend**.

After **26 GENERATIONS**, the **Marquis Piero Antinori** is the leader of this emblematic company, which now crosses the borders of Tuscany, supported by his three daughters: **Albiera, Alegra and Alessia**. This, the first generation made up entirely of women, will take the reins of the vineyard whose mystique began, perhaps, more than 3,000 years ago with a war, an ingenious wooden horse, a long exile and a handful of bright Tuscan grapes.

Twenty-six generations

"In those high hills of Antinori…
a wine so pure that it jumps and shines in the glass."
Francesco Redi, poet of the 17th century,
praised the wines of Antinori

20 hectares located in **the heart of the Chianti Classico.**
On a hillside at **400m** above sea level, among the highest
of the region.

Rocky soils, marine loam rich in **LIMESTONE** from the Eocene
and Miocene geological periods.

About the 1997 Solaia, wine critic Robert
Parker, Jr., said: *"If a Premier Cru of Pauillac were*
made in Tuscany… this (Solaia) would be it!"

History of the ANTINORI family {26 GENERATIONS}

1184
Rinuccio di Antinoro
started producing wine
on the outskirts of Florence

1385
GIOVANNI DI PIERO ANTINORI
joined the **guild of winemakers** in Florence

1506
Niccolo Antinori
ACQUIRES
Palazzo Antinori

1510
The wine was sold
to the local aristocratic families
from the palace
windows

1943
VILLA ANTINORI
was bombed
during the war,
but the family was able to hide
some wine barrels

1970
First harvest of Tignanello,
THE FAMOUS SUPER TUSCAN,
BASED ON SANGIOVESE
mixed with Bordeaux varieties

1978
First vintage of Solaia,
a Super Tuscan
based mainly on
cabernet sauvignon

1986
Piero Antinori
IS NAMED
"Decanter Man of the Year"

2000
Solaia 1997
is named by *Wine Spectator* as the
#1 WINE
among the 100 best wines in the world

FROM *TERROIR* TO BOTTLE

The vineyard is located near Florence, in the Chianti Classico region of Tuscany.

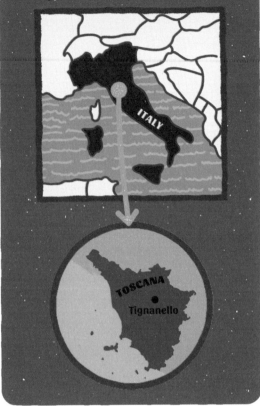

ITALY

TOSCANA
Tignanello

The varieties of the blend

20 % SANGIOVESE

5 % CABERNET FRANC

75 % CABERNET SAUVIGNON

SOLAIA

ANTINORI

The Tignanello Vineyard

(altitude: 320–400 meters above sea level)

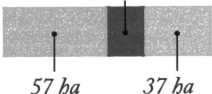

20 ha
SOLAIA WINE

57 ha
TIGNANELLO WINE

37 ha
OLIVE TREES
For the house olive oil

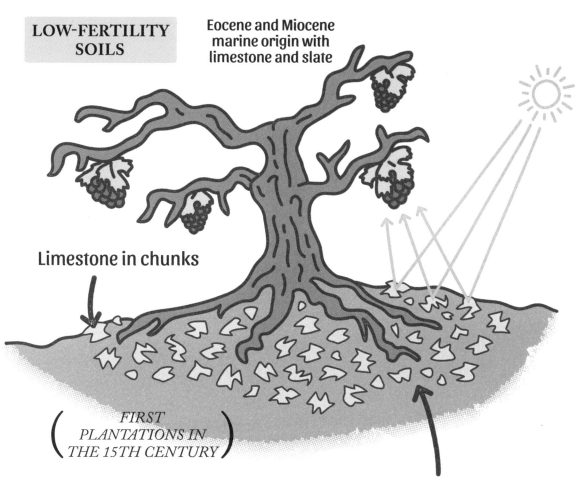

LOW-FERTILITY SOILS

Eocene and Miocene marine origin with limestone and slate

Limestone in chunks

$\left(\begin{array}{c}\textit{FIRST}\\ \textit{PLANTATIONS IN}\\ \textit{THE 15TH CENTURY}\end{array}\right)$

ANTINORI TECHNIQUE
to obtain soft tannins
in Sangiovese
(what they call a "nervous" grape)

They pulverize the limestone and distribute it around each vine trunk to reflect sunlight on the grapes and soften the tannins.

What is a Super Tuscan?

A new breed of Tuscan wines that originated in 1970, when winemakers first blended the local Sangiovese with Bordeaux varieties, such as Cabernet Sauvignon and Merlot.

{ *Other famous Super Tuscans are Tignanello (also by Antinori), Sassicaia, Masseto, Ornellaia and Redigaffi.* }

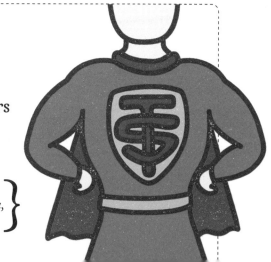

Château d'Yquem

The noble rot

In the twilight, barefoot and trembling, with her hands clasped on her chest, Françoise Josephine de Sauvage d'Yquem closed her eyes and imagined her vineyard in all its splendor.

President Washington's wine

"Wine is a necessity of life for me."
Thomas Jefferson

When Josephine, just 23 years old, was thrown into a damp, dark cell in 1793, for the sole reason of being a French aristocrat, she had the terrible certainty that she would only leave to face the **guillotine**.

Josephine clung to the intimate image of her childhood paradise where her parents, their land and the delicate scent of vineyards became a soft blanket of tranquility that would embrace her forever.

In that cold winter of 1789, the **French Revolution** had lost its way and was out of control. In Paris, for the next two years, nearly **3,000 human** beings would be guillotined, including the owners of Chateau Margaux and Château Lafite, King Louis XVI, Queen Marie-Antoinette, and Robespierre himself, the transcendental leader of the Revolution.

Daguerreotype of Napoleon III, who in 1855 declared Château d'Yquem the only Premier Cru Supérieur in France.

How could a young woman like Josephine, an orphan since the age of 17 and a recent widow, imagine her salvation? She was isolated, vulnerable and condemned without any chance of a fair trial.

However, Françoise Josephine de Sauvage d'Yquem **would go on to live another 60 years**, after having made her vineyards prosper as never before, built on her extraordinary talent for the administration of her domains and a rare capacity for innovation.

Three years after her death, almost as a posthumous recognition of her work, Bordeaux's Official Classification of Wines —which took place for the first time in the framework of the Universal Exhibition of 1855 at the request of the Emperor Napoleon III— declared Château d'Yquem *the only Premier Cru Superieur* in France.

During the 19th century, Josephine's descendants carried on her pioneering vision, and the vineyard continued to grow in reputation, becoming one of the most prestigious in the world.

Shortly after marrying Josephine,
the young Louis-Amédée de Lur-Saluces,
godson of Louis XV and Victoria of France,
falls from his horse and dies instantly.

When an LVMH representative came to Yquem
after Arnault bought shares in the property,

Alexandre told him,
"Yquem is not for sale."

In 1968, the brothers Eugène and Alexandre de Lur-Saluces inherited part of the property of the Lady d'Yquem. Alexandre, being the youngest, only received a small percentage of the land, however.

No matter his small ownership, Alexandre managed the property with tremendous talent, facing several disastrous crops and tremendous financial difficulties.

In 1980, with the brand strengthened again, Alexandre decided to reinvest all the profits and refused to distribute dividends to Eugène and the rest of the **family**. The conflicts of interest reached a peak, and family members began looking for a buyer for this most valuable of properties.

At that time, **Bernard Arnault**, the world's leading luxury brand entrepreneur, owner of the LVMH group (Christian Dior, Givenchy, Louis Vuitton, Hennesy, Moët et Chandon, Veuve Cliquot and Bulgari, among many other brands), was offered a unique and almost unimaginable opportunity to acquire the Château d'Yquem and its vineyards.

YQUEM
ne se vend
PAS!

*Alexandre de Lur-Saluces
refused to sell the winery.*

The disagreements among Josephine's heirs grew. Reports claim that during the dispute, Alexandre, furious, spent thousands of dollars on psychoanalysts and lawyers.

The battle between him and Bernard Arnault, perceived by the French as a contemporary version of **David and Goliath**, provoked fascination throughout France and appeared as a daily family drama in the nation's newspapers.

In 1999, after years of seemingly endless legal battles, Count Alexandre de Lur-Saluces <u>finally ceded and sold some of his shares to his enemy</u> in exchange for the possibility to continue as administrator of the Chateau. As part of the settlement, Alexandre imposed the condition that his relatives be prohibited from entering Château d'Yquem and its vineyards.

In April of that same year, after a ruthless fight drawn to the verge of madness, **Bernard and Alexandre finally toasted the sale... with a glass of Château d'Yquem 1899!**

Alexander reigned as administrator over Yquem until his retirement in 2004.

In 2011, a bottle of Chateau d'Yquem 1811 was sold at the Ritz Hotel for

US$ 117.000

*making it **the most expensive bottle of white wine in history.***

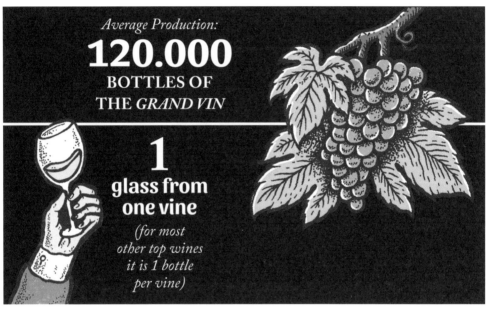

Average Production:

120.000
BOTTLES OF
THE *GRAND VIN*

1
**glass from
one vine**

*(for most
other top wines
it is 1 bottle
per vine)*

Le Sérum

Dior

In 2006,
Dior and Chateau d'Yquem
created a
beauty product
based on the
sap
of the Yquem vines.

An original
**small
stronghold**
exists here,
in the valley of the Ciron River,
since the

★ **XII**th ★
century

IN THE 1980s,
a French
astronaut
AND WINE LOVER
took a bottle of
Château d'Yquem
into **space.**

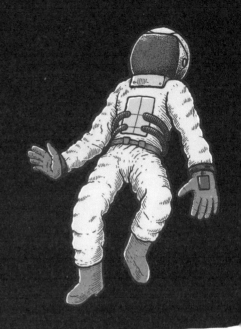

Its
alcohol *and the* **sugar**
content is around   content is around
13,5 %   **125g/l**

(EQUAL PROPORTION OF SUGAR TO A COCA-COLA) →

JEFFERSON

Delighted by a taste of Yquem,
Thomas
Jefferson
paid a fortune for
30 dozen bottles
for his cellar and that of
George Washington.

In the hands of women

*"The Sheriff here is d'Yquem,
Sauternes is the gold,
and the Ciron the Rio Bravo."*
John Wayne

Château d'Yquem is located in the **Sauternes** region, about 40 kilometers southeast of the city of <u>Bordeaux</u>. Its location near the sea gives it a temperate oceanic climate. In the morning, mist invades the pine forests, and, in the evenings, as a climatic counterpoint, the warm winds arrive.

These factors are essential to the rich composition of Yquem's warm and dry soils, thanks to the sand of the upper layers and the humidity of the deeper layers where clay dominates.

This combination of soil and climate allows for the growth of *botrytis cinerea*, the fungus that is the fundamental key in the genesis of the vintage.

The fungus consumes up to 50% of the water in the grapes, thus increasing the concentration of sugars and decreasing the level of acidity. All this happens without the grain breaking, in a natural process that is called **NOBLE ROT**.

The result of this *Noble Rot* is a breathtaking wine, extremely sophisticated and complex. But if in the last stage of maturation the fungus reproduces at a <u>high rate from excessive humidity</u> and not enough sun, it becomes a **lethal** process called Gray Rot. The consequences for the grapes are devastating, and the vintage is suspended —**that year there will be no Château d'Yquem!**

The pruning and vineyard travails are done exclusively by women, thanks to their small and delicate hands, with the goal of obtaining only 10 clusters of grapes per plant. One woman is responsible for each individual plot and charged with the choice of the miraculous "noble" grapes.

FROM *TERROIR* TO BOTTLE

The vineyard is located near the Ciron River in Sauternes, in the region of Bordeaux, France.

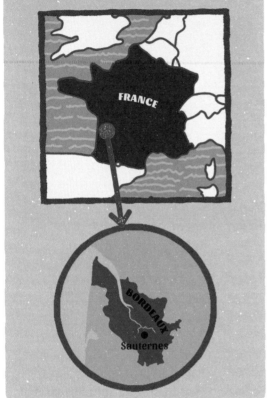

FRANCE

BORDEAUX

● Sauternes

Twenty-five female harvesters, each responsible for a plot, choose the grapes with Noble Rot and discard any grapes with Gray Rot.

↓

The women harvest in 6 passes over a month.

(Women are chosen for their small hands and attention to detail.)

The varieties of the blend:

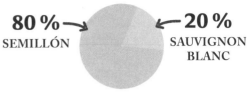

80 % ↘
SEMILLÓN

↙ **20 %**
SAUVIGNON BLANC

↓

HONEY

APRICOTS

SWEET

BROWN WITH TIME

NECTAR

FIGS

Château d'Yquem
Sauternes

SAUTERNES

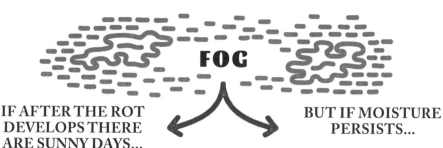

FOG

IF AFTER THE ROT DEVELOPS THERE ARE SUNNY DAYS...

BUT IF MOISTURE PERSISTS...

The fungus is produced by the humidity of the night mist, but sunny days are essential for drying the grapes and curbing excessive rot (which is harmful).

{ FUNGUS *BOTRYTIS CINEREA* }

If it rains or the grapes are not healthy or ripe, gray rot develops, giving the grapes a horrible taste. When gray rot occurs, Château d'Yquem wine is not made for that year.

This is the
Noble Rot
(pourriture noble)

Gray rot = bad

The grapes look rotten <u>BUT</u> produce the most highly coveted white wine, which can last more than 100 years.

(*The fungus generates holes in the clusters that allow the moisture to escape.*)

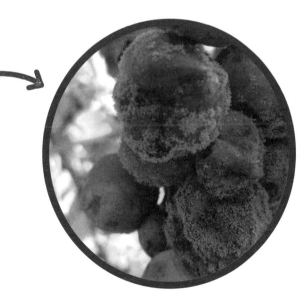

Dehydration produces increased sugars and compounds that add complexity and longevity to the wine.

Dehydrated grapes covered by a fungus that looks like **ash (cinerea)**.

Two small children depart from a Chilean port bound for Spain.

The flavors of history

"Opportunities to find
deeper powers within ourselves
come when life seems most challenging."
<u>*Joseph Campbell*</u>

On an icy morning in 1870, two children hold hands as their ship embarks towards Europe from a Chilean port. One is 14 years old and the other is 12.

They are alone for the first time, and their hands tremble: no family member will accompany them during the trip that will cross the ocean for more than two long months.

When they take their first steps on deck, the children immediately turn anxiously to lean on the railing, looking for a last view of their parents among the crowd gathered in the harbor.

"The two of them crossed the ocean," says great-granddaughter <u>María José López de Heredia</u>, heiress to one of the most prestigious wineries in Spain, "and we keep the precious letters that were sent to their mother, telling her all about the boat journey." They were letters from two children with a maturity more typical of a 40-year-old than of children their age.

Carlista soldier

Their parents had sent them to Orduña, in Spain's Basque Country, to study in a Jesuit school. But only two years later, the **Third Carlist War** broke out. A civil war that left tens of thousands of dead raged intensely in Navarre, Catalonia, and in the Basque provinces.

The two children managed to escape from their school to join the fighting because "the Carlist spirit burned too intensely in their hearts."

But shortly afterwards they were **TAKEN PRISONERS AND DEPORTED** to France.

"Without more heaven than the stars, without more consolation than that of God, our Lord, they had us walking day and night until we crossed the border," wrote Rafael Lopez de Heredia y Landeta to his mother. This 16-year-old adolescent would one day found the mythical winery **Viña Tondonia**, on the right bank of the river Ebro.

His great-granddaughter María José says that Rafael decided to study International Trade in France, with money that his parents sent him from **CHILE**. And he received very good grades...

Elizabethan
Soldier

So much so that a few months later, near Bayonne, he was hired to keep the accounts of a company that traded in wines. When bankruptcy surprised them, and the owners fled to avoid their creditors, Don Rafael saw a golden opportunity.

Two of the creditors were residents of Haro, in La Rioja Alta, the neighborhood that today, next to Jerez and Oporto, holds the highest **concentration of wineries** in the world.

Don Rafael moved to Haro, and the creditors immediately offered him a job to stay and manage the winery. It must have been destiny dictating that the child who had fatefully crossed the Atlantic by the hand of his little brother would never again return to Chile.

The **RIOJAN WINERIES** had begun to multiply in 1863 as a result of the devastating phylloxera plague that had attacked the vineyards of Burgundy, then Bordeaux, and finally all of France (such was the catastrophe that it took more than 30 years to overcome). During the ensuing **"GOLDEN AGE OF RIOJA,"** between 1877 and 1890, the region's vineyards would quadruple their production

Don Rafael built a lookout in the English style, above all the other buildings, to be able to observe every corner of his vineyards.

Many vineyards flourished in La Rioja after the phylloxera plague attacked the vines in France.

Realizing that he was again facing a great opportunity, Don Rafael began to look for the ideal location to plant his own vineyard. Then one day he reached the lands of Tondonia.

At that time, many Alsatian wine producers had traveled to Rioja to find **vineyards that could replace their famous vineyards in France**, ravaged by phylloxera. The Alsatians would teach Don Rafael how to make good wine. And the best producers of Bordeaux would advise him on how to buy the best vines.

Viña Tondonia was founded in 1877, and in a short time it would become a legend.

Almost ten years later, when the construction of the house was being carried out in the middle of the property, Don Rafael also built an **English-style lookout**, high above all the other buildings.

Everyone imagined that his goal was to show the world the huge sign that announced "Viña Tondonia." But what Don Rafael was really trying to do was to have a high place from which to oversee his whole property and each one of his vines.

"In Rioja they say that 1964 is the harvest of the century. I call it a miraculous harvest because it does not seem to grow old over time."

María José López de Heredia

Much had happened since that fateful day in the distant Latin American port when Don Rafael felt the **trembling hand of his younger brother**.

Today, 14 children and hundreds of nephews, grandchildren and great-grandchildren later, Don Rafael's inheritance has become something much more important than a vineyard. His legacy is a true monument to a tale of survival, tenacity and ingenuity.

Don Rafael's great-granddaughter María José affirms that **"ONLY THE CLASSIC LASTS IN TIME,"** and side by side with her siblings she continues a philosophy of artisan winemaking that dates back more than 140 years. For this reason, the traditional cultivation of the vineyard is still used "en vaso" (bushvine), and not "in trellis," as do most of the other Riojan vineyards that rely on a wire fence supported by poles. María José knows about tradition: "For ten years we hired an anthropologist to put order into the family archives. Just the correspondence occupies a pile of volumes, 500 pages each. I am planning to read each and everyone of them, even if it means that I am unable to finish Joyce's *Ulysses*."

The history of <u>LA RIOJA</u> as **a mayor wine producer** *starts in the* **XIXth century,** *when Bordeaux producers* went out in search of **new farmland after the phylloxera plague** *destroyed most of* **the French vineyards.**

Cultivated vines **"on trellis"** are guided vertically, *supported on a fence of wire* **on posts.**

Cultivated vines **"en vaso" (bushvines),** have no artificial support and, *need much more intensive care and constant attention* **because they develop fewer leaves.** *But the ones they have are much more* **exposed to the sun.** Thus, in addition to protecting the soil surrounding the vine, **THE LEAVES PROTECT THE CLUSTERS** from excessive dehydration.

The cellars ARE **15 meters underground,** which helps maintain the temperature at **12 ºC** <u>*without the need for electrical cooling.*</u>

While the minimum aging of a **RIOJA GRAN RESERVA** is 6 years, **Viña Tondonia** *is aged in barrels* between **10** and **20** years *before being released for sale.*

Vines grown "en vaso" (bushvines).

FROM *TERROIR* TO BOTTLE

The vineyard is located near Haro, in the region of La Rioja, Spain.

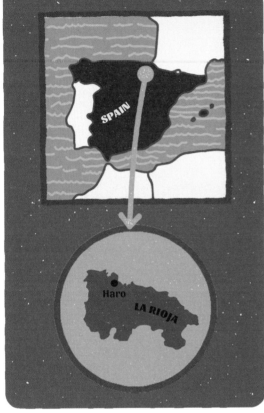

SPAIN

Haro — LA RIOJA

The varieties of the blend

75 %
TEMPRANILLO

5 %
MAZUELO

15 %
GARNACHA

5 %
GRACIANO

VINOS FINOS
RIOJA

30

HARO

FUNDADA EN 1877

VIÑA
TONDONIA

The river Ebro

Its surroundings are home to many animals, including wild ducks, European storks, herons, partridges, foxes, rabbits and wild boars that stroll through the vineyard.

TONDÓN *COMES FROM THE LATIN* "ROUND"

and alludes to the curve that takes the river Ebro around the Tondonia vineyard.

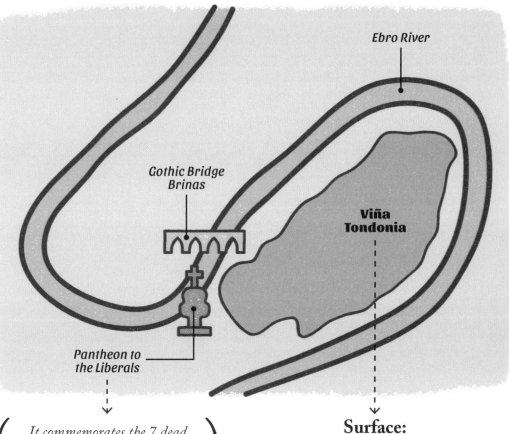

Ebro River

Gothic Bridge
Brinas

Viña
Tondonia

Pantheon to
the Liberals

(*It commemorates the 7 dead*
in the anti-Carlista fight of 1834.)

Surface:
100 ha

(Altitude 438–489 meters above sea level)

**Lots of 100 m² and mostly bush vines
in the style of the first plantations.**

Vines "en vaso"
(bushvines)

without wire support

*Most of the world's vineyards
are planted on a wire and on a
vertical trellis, making
this a very traditional style.*

FIRST
PLANTATIONS
IN 1913

*SOILS OF ALLUVIAL ORIGIN
CLAYS ON CALCAREOUS*

★ NAPA VALLEY, CALIFORNIA ★

HARLAN ESTATE

Harlan Estate

The California adventurer

Bill Harlan, possessor of an adventurous spirit, decided to travel to Africa on a motorcycle. Later, he would end up owning one of the most important vineyards in the United States.

A history
of the future

"A person often meets his destiny
on the road he took to avoid it."
Jean de La Fontaine

What can a man, who travels on a motorcycle throughout **AFRICA**, studies Communication and Political Science in California, plays **poker** for a living —while sleeping in a casino hotel— and learns to pilot **planes** before deciding to start selling them, be searching for?

The answer may seem incomprehensible: land, a vineyard for his family, and **200 years of great crops producing** one of the best aromas in the world.

To understand this mystery, we must first know that long before embarking on his adventures, Bill Harlan had felt an undeniable love for the gardens of his childhood. And that child, **the son of a butcher and a housewife**, felt the greatest delight in the world when he <u>rode his bicycle on a vineyard road</u>. During those endless afternoons, he could never have suspected that he was also passing through the very substance of his future, to which he would return after moving away to its antipodes. It was as if his life had always orbited, mysteriously, around those near-forgotten vineyards and childhood afternoons.

NEW YORK CITY DEPUTY POLICE COMMISSIONER JOHN A. LEACH (RIGHT) WATCHING AGENTS POUR LIQUOR INTO SEWER FOLLOWING A RAID

Between the late 1950s and the early 1960s, American wine enthusiasts began to move into the **NAPA VALLEY** area, home to the few vineyards that had survived the **alcohol prohibition of the 1920s**. They came upon small towns that felt frozen in time and a landscape so striking that it would become the promised land for those who, like **WILLIAM HARLAN**, were looking for a fertile spot in which to build a future.

The founding of the **Mondavi Winery** in 1966 was the first step in a California desire to produce wines in the United States that reached the quality of the famous vineyards of Bordeaux and beyond.

36 DRY RAIDS START CITY-WIDE ROUND-UP

100 Federal Agents Open Drive on Speakeasies Listed in Street-by-Street Census.

Uptown Bars Exhaust Supplies of Liquor and Shut Up.		Suburban Cutups and Novices Have Hot Time On Short Beers.

The so-called dry law was in force in the United States between 1920 and 1933, and prohibited the sale, import, export, manufacture and transportation of alcoholic beverages.

Harlan was dazzled by this fact and Mondavi's mission. However, he had to first find his way in the world to understand that his future in Napa was ineluctable.

After a long journey around the globe, Harlan discovered, among other things, his ability to do business: He was a co-founder of Pacific Union, one of the most important real estate companies on the West Coast of the United States, with a **millionaire collection of properties**.

This enterprise made possible everything that awaited him. And what awaited him…it was the life of a farmer!

Competing with the French vineyards felt like an **impossible dream**.

"The most important gift I received in my entire life was an invitation from Robert Mondavi to visit the vineyards of Bordeaux and Burgundy in 1980.

That experience offered me a very different view of time... these French properties endured for hundreds of years and countless generations. That is when I realized that what I really wanted was to make a Premier Cru, but in California."

William Harlan

If there was **a possibility in a million**, and if someone was passionately motivated to try it, it would take land. And experts. And discipline. And courage. And a tremendous amount of investment. But, above all, a **PLAN** would be necessary —and not a short-term one. If the making of a Bordeaux Premier Cru such as Château Lafite Rothschild or Romanée-Conti of Burgundy took centuries, they would need a similar and equivalent objective…for the next two centuries. And that was exactly what William Harlan dreamed about: **MAKING HISTORY**.

In the Old World, great wines, he noted, are produced on slopes. That is why Bill Harlan decided to carve his future in the sloping hills of the Mayacamas Mountains, west of Martha's Vineyard, where he bought his first 16 hectares of land in 1984. Harlan first grew 1½ hectares in 1985, seven more in the next two years, and the last in 1990.

Robert Mondavi and William Harlan, in a French vineyard.

Shortly thereafter, thanks to deep soil studies, long days working together with a team of experts that was growing month by month and an investment of energy and money that he never imagined possible, the Harlan Estate unveiled **its first 200 cases of Cabernet Sauvignon and 200 more of Chardonnay**.

But Harlan had achieved something much more important than a first vintage; he had taken the first step in the production of a wine that would soon compete with <u>the most celebrated in the world</u>.

The quality, however, was not yet up to Harlan's expectations.

It wasn't until 1996, when the 1990, 1991, 1992, 1993 harvests were bottled and the 1994 was in barrel, that Harlan and his team finally decided to sit down with a wine critic to savor the 1990 harvest for the first time.

The result of this encounter is the beginning of the legend: **they had achieved the first year of immortality**.

Now, William Harlan could take a deep breath in his Napa Valley, and experience once again, with that same childhood delight, the sleepy fields that hid the treasure of today: a once-hidden world, now bursting, thanks to his will, his **determination** and a **certain madness**.

Harlan's 1994 crop was the first to receive 100 points from wine critic Robert Parker, Jr.

A dynasty is born

Harlan says that it took him 20 years to earn the first dollar selling the Harlan Estate label, because of the **costs**, **labor** and **time** invested in its production.

He says he has a **PLAN** for the **next 200 years** to create a European-style **wine dynasty** in the tradition of the <u>Rothschilds</u> and the <u>Antinoris</u>.

Harlan owns the **Napa Valley Reserve**, a private club with about 500 members from 37 states and 11 countries. **For an initial down payment** of approximately **$155,000**, members can enjoy great wine and culinary events, educational trips to vineyards around the world and the <u>use of the local</u> <u>infrastructure</u> —in addition to receiving a substantial annual allocation of cases of Napa wine.

A bottle of
Harlan
cabernet sauvignon
SELLS BETWEEN

$400
AND
$1200

depending on the year of harvest.

WILLIAM HARLAN
is also the ***founder*** *of*
MEADOWOOD RESORT,
the most famous hotel in
Napa Valley,
which has a
restaurant
that has been awarded
3 stars
by the *Michelin Guide.*

Bill Harlan met his wife, **Deborah Beck,**
ON A BLIND DATE *in 1985. They have* **TWO CHILDREN**
who today **work alongside them** *on the property:*
William, born in 1987, and **Amanda,** born in 1989.

FROM *TERROIR* TO BOTTLE

The vineyard is located in the Napa Valley, California.

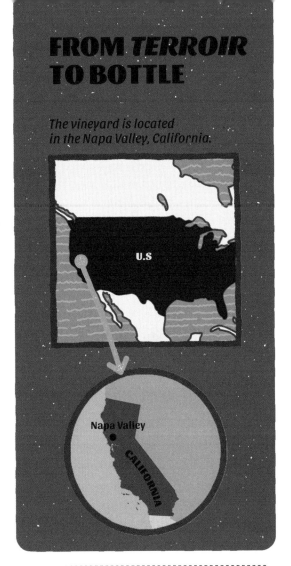

U.S

Napa Valley

CALIFORNIA

The varieties of the blend

CABERNET FRANC

MERLOT

CABERNET SAUVIGNON

PETIT VERDOT

(The exact percentage of each variety is decided at each harvest.)

Cult Wines

California wines that are produced in small quantities are hard to come by and are often auctioned off for thousands of dollars.

{ *Other cult wines besides Harlan include Screaming Eagle, Sine Qua Non, Scarecrow, Araujo, Grace Family Vineyards, Dominus, Dalla Valle and Peter Michael.* }

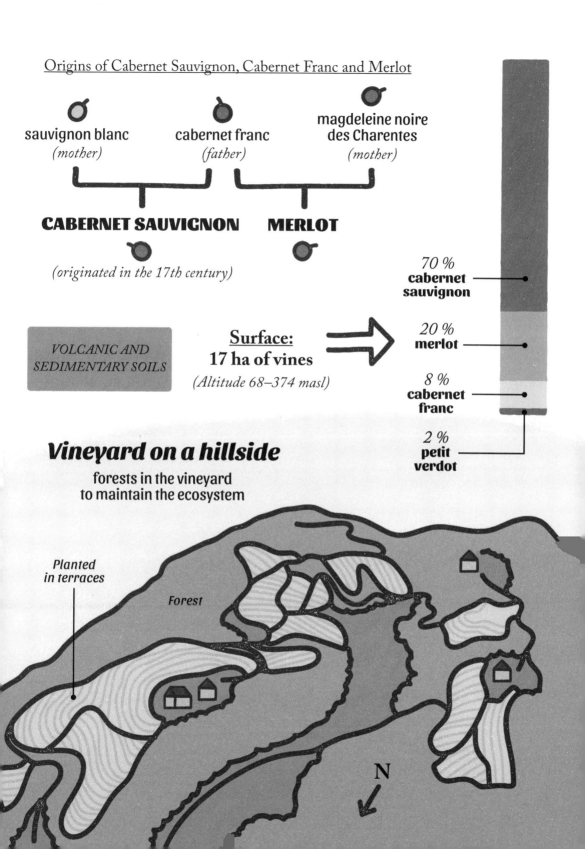

Origins of Cabernet Sauvignon, Cabernet Franc and Merlot

sauvignon blanc
(mother)

cabernet franc
(father)

magdeleine noire
des Charentes
(mother)

CABERNET SAUVIGNON

MERLOT

(originated in the 17th century)

VOLCANIC AND
SEDIMENTARY SOILS

Surface:
17 ha of vines
(Altitude 68–374 masl)

70 %
cabernet sauvignon

20 %
merlot

8 %
cabernet franc

2 %
petit verdot

Vineyard on a hillside

forests in the vineyard
to maintain the ecosystem

Planted in terraces

Forest

N

Romanée-Conti

A world heritage wine

LE
SECRET DU ROI

"No one knew how to entertain
with more elegance and subtlety
than the prince of Conti,"
maintained Madame de Genlis,
the French writer who supported
the Revolution shortly after.

Chronicle of the war of the vines

How many things can a human being want?
How many can he really obtain?
And above all: What does he really possess?

Louis François de Bourbon,

<u>prince of Conti</u>, is remembered for one of the most remarkable vineyards in history, the legendary Romanée-Conti in Burgundy.

The prince possessed everything that any man of his day might desire: intelligence, culture, seductiveness, a noble title, and a talent for combat, politics and the arts… and as if all of that were not enough, he led **"LE SECRET DU ROI,"** the first **secret intelligence service of the French** monarchy. The prince was a true James Bond of 18th-century European espionage.

Like every hero, the prince had an <u>arch-enemy</u>: **MADAME DE POMPADOUR**, King Louis XV's favorite.

In 1764, the artist Michel-Barthélemy Ollivier portrayed the prince and his surroundings in the oil on canvas above, titled "English tea in the hall of the four mirrors of the temple, with the whole court of the Prince Conti listening to the young Mozart," currently in the Louvre Museum.

She and the prince had been the two people closest to the king…and the most influential people in his court. But to their political enmity was added the prince's desire to become king of Poland, as had been his grandfather. It was a desire opposed by "La Pompadour," and the prince of Conti never became king of Poland.

According to legend, a final battle between the two for power and sway over the king of France was inevitable, and could not happen on any other terrain than at the Romanée vineyard.

It was a battle without armies or ammunition, a last face-off between two sworn enemies, a battle for the acquisition of the famous Burgundian property, surrounded by its exquisite vineyards.

The Prince of Conti

The prince would end up buying the land for more than **10 times the value** of any other vineyard in the region, and would one-up La Pompadour by purchasing it secretly through an <u>intermediary</u>.

And so, it would not be the Polish crown that made the prince the legend that would span almost four centuries to reach these pages.

It would be, rather, his spirit reflected in those vines. Nothing but earth and grapes —but without a doubt the most magical and memorable soils and vines in history.

So magical that the prince **NEVER SOLD A SINGLE BOTTLE** of his Romanée wine. The almost 2,000 bottles that were produced each year were consumed at innumerable dinners, concerts and evenings with artists and politicians in the prince's legendary salons.

When the prince died in **1776**, his son inherited the vineyard and the name Conti was added to the Domaine's name. But in a tragic twist shortly afterwards, the <u>French Revolution</u> confiscated the property and declared it **NATIONAL PATRIMONY**.

Years later, in 1794, it was **auctioned** off to the highest bidder.

> # "It is almost a hallmark of Domaine de la Romanée-Conti wines: They are instantly recognizable by their exotic opulence."
>
> *Hugh Johnson*

After passing through many hands, the property was acquired in 1869 by <u>Jacques-Marie Duvault-Blochet</u>, an **ancestor** to the de Villaines, initiating the current family's ownership, joined decades later by the Leroy family.

This union of surnames, de Villaine and Leroy, continues to this day as they share Domaine de La Romanée-Conti in equal parts.

Not satisfied with owning the most famous property in Burgundy, **Aubert de Villaine** embarked on a mission to have the vineyards of his beloved Burgundy named a **UNESCO World Heritage Site**.

In 2010, **Aubert de Villaine** and a group of fellow producers presented the candidacy for the Burgundian domains between Dijon to the north and the appellation Marangues to the south.

Aubert de Villaine presented the Burgundy Vineyard candidacy to UNESCO in 2010.

Burgundy won World Heritage Site designation at the Bonn UNESCO meeting in 2015.

The Romanée-Conti vineyard is today one of the **SMALLEST PROPERTIES** in France. Only **1.8 HECTARES** of vineyards produce about 5,000 bottles a year of a wine that can cost more than **$10,000** per bottle —even those from a recent harvest— but still far from the price paid for a "Millésime" (vintage) 1945: $100,000.

It has been almost **800 years** since the abbot of Saint Vivant acquired the first two hectares of this legendary parcel of land in **1232.**

THE AVERAGE
PRICE
of a
BOTTLE
of the current vintage of
ROMANÉE-CONTI
Is approximately
$14,800

The vineyard was
planted
for the first time in the
XIIIth
CENTURY.

It has been in the hands of
the Villaine
FAMILY
since the year
1869.

The other world-famous wine
FROM DOMAINE DE LA ROMANÉE-CONTI
(the name of the winery and the vineyard)
*comes from **La Tâche vineyard.***

LA TÂCHE
is known as a
MASCULINE
wine

and

ROMANÉE-CONTI
is known as a more
FEMININE
wine

A privileged inheritance

The **1.8 GOLDEN** hectares next to the village of Vosne-Romanée are blessed with the perfect climate to make a wine of excellence.

The **Romanée-Conti vineyard** consists of a small well-drained hillside with east and southeast orientation, 240 meters above sea level.

Its **soils** are composed of <u>limestone</u> and are rich in <u>iron</u>.

The selection of Pinot Noir "très fin" plants inherited from the old Romanée-Conti property is an incomparable **genetic inheritance**, *with a delicacy and complexity that ensure the purity of the wines produced here.*

The **acidity** of a wine with this heritage allows it to evolve favorably for decades.

It is an **ORGANICALLY** farmed vineyard with an average vine age of 45 years.

Biodynamic techniques have been practiced here since 2007.

The Romanée-Conti **1985** was awarded the highly prized 100 points by Robert Parker, Jr., the most prestigious wine critic in the world.

Only one
variety

100 %
PINOT
NOIR

MONOPOLE
2004

ROMI

AMX CHILE DU DOMANE DE LA DOMANE COM
MONOPOLE AOUSNE ROMANÉE ICOTÉ DOR SUMON

ROMANÉE-CONTI

APPELLATION ROMANÉE-CONTI CONTROLÉE

663 Boolaltes Pinslos

OILER 01775
ANNÉE 2004

FROM *TERROIR* TO BOTTLE

The vineyard is located on the Côte de Nuits (Côte d'Or), near the town of Dijon, in the region of Burgundy.

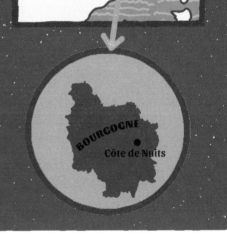

FRANCE

BOURGOGNE

Côte de Nuits

LATE 19TH-CENTURY
**attack of the phylloxera plague
on the vineyards of France.**

⇓

Almost all of the vines were
replanted using a phylloxera-resistant
American vine rootstock with a
grafted European *vitis vinifera* vine.

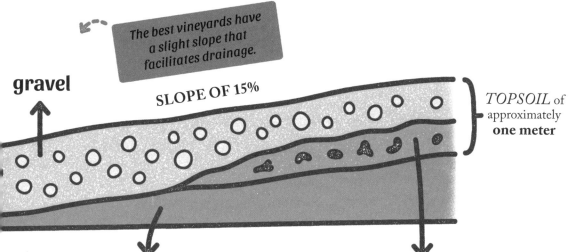

The best vineyards have a slight slope that facilitates drainage.

gravel

SLOPE OF 15%

TOPSOIL of approximately **one meter**

calcaire à entroques
Clay lime of Jurassic origin

It is said that the best Pinot Noir *wines come from calcareous soils.*

Bed of marine fossils
rich in limestoneo
(ostrea acuminata)

MARINE FOSSILS

THE ROMANÉE-CONTI VINEYARD WAS NOT REPLANTED UNTIL 1945.

Instead of replanting with selected clones of one, two or three plants, Romanée-Conti decided to plant a more diverse selection of dozens of different plants called "populations."

Aubert de Villaine believes that this genetic diversity is important for the quality of Pinot Noir from the Romanée-Conti.

Average age of the vines: 40 years

High plant density: **10,000 to 14,000 per hectare.**

Wehlener Sonnenuhr
A German clock

The sweetness of time

*"Great wine requires
a madman to grow the vine,
a wise man to watch over it,
a lucid poet to make it
and a lover to drink it."*

Salvador Dalí

In 1971 a **passionate wine collector** decided to buy two cases of the famous Joh. Jos. Prüm. His purpose was to open a bottle every year, taste the evolution of the wine and savor the impact of **time** over its character. But it is possible to think that what this man truly wanted was to understand his own evolution in time, to perceive through his palate and the wine his own transformation.

Katharina Prüm, the owner of one of the most <u>famous vineyards in Germany</u>, met this passionate man. And her appreciation of what her own family had accomplished across so many centuries in the vineyards of Wehlen was never the same.

"The development of wine is unpredictable... as unpredictable as a human being," says Katharina.

In addition to making an excellent wine, the challenge of the Prüm family was to cultivate on the steepest and possibly most difficult slopes in the world. Without a doubt, the Joh. Jos. Prüm owes much of its reputation to those **PRIVILEGED 14 HECTARES**, located in the heart of Germany. More than **800 YEARS** ago, the Prüm family settled in Wehlen, in the valleys of the **MOSEL**.

"My role is not to change the wines of Joh. Jos. Prüm."

Katharina Prüm

Five centuries later, Prüm was transformed into a cellar, and Sebastian Alois Prüm began the mythical and almost inhuman work of farming and harvesting grapes from the steep vines of Wehlener Sonnenuhr. At the same time, another legend was born in the region when **sundials** (Sonnenhur) were built on the slopes leading down to the Mosel River. These clocks would mark the work hours on those <u>dangerous slopes</u>, bringing relief to workers at the end of a day of patient and arduous labor.

The great leap for the Prüm family came in 1911, when <u>Johann Josef Prüm</u> transformed wine production, and quality rose exponentially. Ten years later, his son Sebastian took the reins, and it was under Sebastian's leadership that, during the 1930s and '40s, the Prüm **RIESLING** developed **a unique style**, different from everyone else's in the region.

The vineyard workers eagerly watch the sundial, waiting for the end of the day.

But how can we truly define the difference that marks J.J. Prüm from all the other vineyards in the valleys of the Mosel? Is it possible to explain that particular magic?

The difference starts, as always, with the selection of parcels. The techniques and daily care of the vineyard are important, of course. But there is much more: the harvest must be started as late as possible, the grapes selected through individual scrutiny…and time. **Time for the vines to express their best potential; time to assimilate the climate, minerals, water, sugar; time to innovate along with the evolution of the earth** —and also time for a human being who decides his destiny to really understand it.

When Sebastian died in 1969, his son Manfred understood the family's past, present, and future in all its greatness and followed his father's lead. Years later, Manfred's daughter Katharina, with equal devotion, joined him to preserve the legacy of the family holdings.

"I do not like the expression 'winemakers,' because it seems to indicate that one is 'making' the wine. And it is not like this; the only thing we do is accompany it. We only try to express what nature offers us. And once we find that ideal balance of elements, we hope to intervene, in a way, as little as possible," says Katharina Prüm.

Today, both Katharina and her passionate wine customer, who continues his tradition of sampling one bottle a year of his valuable collection, to know the evolution of wine and of himself, know that every harvest, every day and every encounter generate equally unpredictable consequences.

It is in that same state of uncertainty and anxious expectation that the beauty, magic and potential greatness of a vineyard lies…and its **future**.

The taste of gold

The property is located on slate soils that seem impenetrable. The fact that you can grow a vine under such adverse conditions is practically miraculous.

The wines are aged in **TRADITIONAL 1000-LITER BARRELS**, and the winemaking practices are practically identical to those used by the winery's <u>founder</u>, Johann Josef Prüm.

No one has earned the <u>distinction</u> of "Best Riesling" from the prestigious **Gault Millau** food and wine magazine more often than J.J. Prüm.

The most famous HARVESTS are: **1949, 1959, 1976, 1988, 1997, 1999, 2000 and 2001.**

The prestigious German wine sommelier Frank Kämmer has said that J.J. Prüm resembles a prima ballerina in its "precision, elegance and grace."

Riesling wines
of Germany are divided into
six categories
**DEPENDING ON THE
MATURITY OF THE GRAPES,**
from lower *(Kabinet)*
to greater ripeness
(Trockenbeerenauslese).

*Kabinet wines are the only ones
that tend to be completely
dry (not sweet).*

MATURITY

THE **6** CATEGORIES ARE

Kabinet
(lower maturity)

Spätlese

Auslese

Beerenauslese

Eiswein

Trockenbeerenauslese
(greater maturity and sweeter)

The average price of
A BOTTLE
of this **Riesling**
is more than
$5,000.

JOH. JOS. PRÜM
is one of the
most famous
RIESLINGS
in Europe.

The wines of Joh. Jos. Prüm
are famous for their
matchstick aromas
and their ability to
age.

FROM *TERROIR* TO BOTTLE

The vineyard is located in the village of Wehlen on the Mosel River in southwestern Germany.

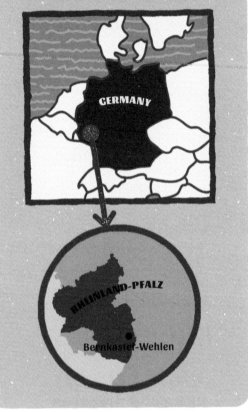

GERMANY

RHEINLAND-PFALZ

Bernkastel-Wehlen

Wehlener Sonnenuhr

Village name   sundial clock

22 ha and 200 plots with many different owners
Joh. Jos. Prüm parcel in Wehlener Sonnenuhr: 5 ha

The name Prüm is centenary in the area of the Mosel River. There are 7 wineries with the name Prüm but only one Joh. Jos. Prüm.

Only one variety

100 % RIESLING

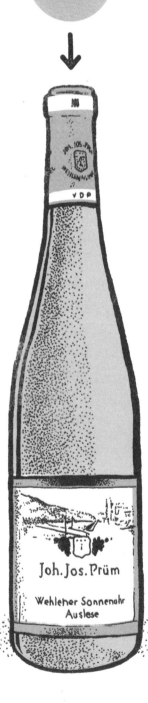

Joh. Jos. Prüm

Wehlener Sonnenuhr
Auslese

Aged Sweet Wines

Sugar acts as a preservative for wine. That is why the sweet wines of the Mosel, the Sauternes of France and ports are known for their ability to age.

Riesling parents

wild vine   traminer

gouais blanc
(also one of the parents of chardonnay)

the other parent
(unknown)

RIESLING

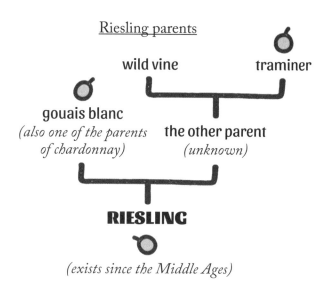

(exists since the Middle Ages)

Age of the vines: 80 years

↓

UNGRAFTED
(without American vine rootstock)

Mosel River

Gray slate floors
from the Devonian period

SLOPE 70%

Photo: © Weingut J.J. Prüm

THE FAMOUS DEVONIAN SLATE FLOORS

It is said that the intense minerality and floral aromas of the Riesling from this area are due to these soils.

Leflaive Montrachet

The queen of wines

"Being at the property in September, for the harvest, was the best moment of my life," said Anne-Claude Leflaive. "It was inspiring to work outdoors and later meet with all the workers to sing and drink good wine."

The girl who was in love with vines

"Anthroposophy does not seek to impart knowledge. It seeks to awaken life."

Rudolf Steiner

In the summer of **1973**, **Anne-Claude Leflaive**, age 17, traveled to her family's vineyard in Burgundy with the same excitement she experienced every year. It felt as if she were heading to her own little paradise of sun and grapes, not knowing that someday it would become her destiny.

This fate would not reveal itself to Anne-Claude until much later, surprising her with a unique challenge.

Anne-Claude's uncle Jo was not happy to see her working in the vineyards: "You should not work in the vineyard with the employees. **You're a Leflaive**. It is not appropriate."

It was Vincent, Anne-Claude's father, who gave his support and allowed her to become involved in the day-to-day of life of the Leflaive vineyards. That year of working the vineyards gave Anne the confidence she would later need to revolutionize the property with her ideas on **BIODYNAMICS**.

The pest phylloxera wreaked havoc on Europe's vineyards.

The Leflaives settled in Burgundy in 1717. But the family's prestige as winemakers began later with **JOSEPH LEFLAIVE** (1870–1953), a naval engineer who operated a factory in Saint Etienne and purchased 25 hectares of vineyards in 1905.

In the early 20th century, Burgundian vineyards could be bought at a very low cost, thanks to the devastation wrought by the <u>phylloxera</u> plague, the scourge of an **insect parasite** that causes the death of the grape plant in only 3 years.

In 1920, Joseph began to **replant his property** and sell the wine under his own brand. After his death in 1953, his children **VINCENT AND JOSEPH, JR.**, continued to improve the quality of their wines, positioning the vineyards as some of the most important in Burgundy.

The **true revolution** would come with Anne-Claude Leflaive, however. She had studied economics in Paris and traveled the world with her husband, Christian Jacques, a navigational instructor and the father of her three daughters. After finishing her studies, Anne devoted herself to teaching.

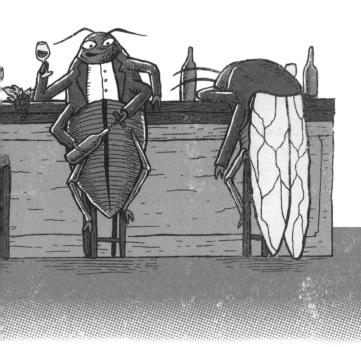

One day, after living in Morocco and Ivory Coast for some time, Anne suddenly felt the **urgent need** to return to her family in France. She immediately applied to study **oenology** at the University of Dijon.

In 1990 Anne moved with her family to Puligny-Montrachet and began to manage Domaine Leflaive <u>with her cousin Olivier</u>. The revolution began with a **BRILLIANT IDEA**: biodynamics.

The harvests of 1987 and 1988 had been heavily criticized, and the property seemed to have lost its course. **RUDOLPH STEINER'S** ideas on biodynamic agriculture seemed to Anne the only possible solution to their vineyards' stagnation.

But biodynamics was not only a method of cultivation and harvesting. It was much more than that: It was a philosophy of life. For many in the region, however, it was also almost a sacrilege. And so it was for her cousin Olivier, according to Anne. The subject became a great source of conflict between the two of them.

Still, Anne pressed on, **experimenting** with her new methods for 3 years, producing wines using both biodynamic and traditional techniques.

"I knew it was the future of the planet... because it was a way to combat the pollution occurring not only on the earth and its atmosphere, but also in humans.

Chemical pesticides had ended life in the vineyard soils. And the wines were full of that chemistry."

Anne-Claude Leflaive (1956-2015)

The results were clear: Soil life was transformed with biodynamics. The health of the vines increased and the improvement in quality was evident.

But Oliver would not be swayed, and the **break** with her cousin proved inevitable. In 1994 a separation of properties allowed Anne to devote herself wholeheartedly to her vineyards and transform them forever.

In 1997 Anne invited celebrated **wine experts** from Corney & Barrow to sample two glasses of wine. Both glasses were from the **same vineyard** and vintage: 1996 Puligny Montrachet Clavoillon. One glass held wine produced through traditional methods and the other held wine made biodynamically.

The experts were unanimous: The glass of biodynamic wine was **clearly superior**.

From that year on, the entire Domaine Leflaive crop was transformed to biodynamic farming, and Anne became a **TIRELESS FIGHTER** against pesticides in the vineyard.

Biodynamic agriculture encompasses all aspects of viticulture: ecological, economic and social.

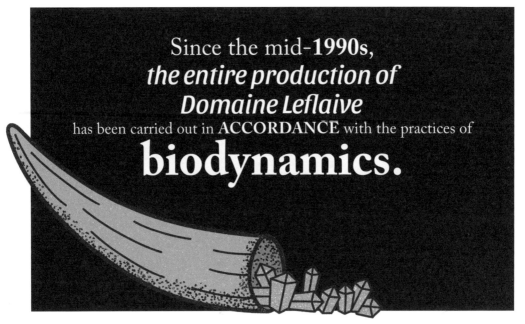

Since the mid-**1990s,**
the entire production of
Domaine Leflaive
has been carried out in ACCORDANCE with the practices of
biodynamics.

The vineyard
Le Montrachet
was declared a
GRAND CRU

in **1937.**

IN LE MONTRACHET
the only variety
that is allowed
to be planted is
Chardonnay.

Domaine Leflaive
Le Montrachet
is the most
expensive
Chardonnay
in the world:
the price of
A BOTTLE
varies between

$5,000

and **$40.000**
depending on the vintage.

The first
vineyard
WAS <u>PLANTED</u> IN
Montrachet
IN THE
XIIIth
CENTURY.

Domaine Leflaive is one of the only
wine properties that still
fully incorporates
THE WORKERS
during harvest.

(Each year, 60 people not only harvest the grapes of the Leflaive
vineyards, but have breakfast, lunch and dinner and sleep
on the property, as it was done in ancient times.)
AND THEY DRINK THE BEST CHARDONNAY IN THE WORLD.

Life in
the vineyard

*"The sun, with all those planets depending on it,
is able to ripen a handful of grapes
as if it had nothing else to do in the universe."*
Galileo Galilei

Biodynamics is the study of the biological processes behind living things. In turn, biodynamic agriculture is a way of understanding farming of the land within an **ECOSYSTEM**, according to the theories of Rudolf Steiner, the founder of anthroposophy.

Biodynamics seeks to **connect the earthly and cosmic processes** that affect life on earth. Biodynamics considers plants as living beings that need not only the energy, water and nutrients they absorb from the different layers of the earth, but also a connection with the rhythms of the sun and moon. The combination of all these elements constitutes the heritage of living organisms on earth.

> # "To truly know the world, look deeply within your own being; to truly know yourself, take real interest in the world."
>
> *Rudolf Steiner*

That is why in biodynamics it is essential to avoid anything that disrupts the **natural development** of the earth's <u>balance</u>, such as the use of pesticides, industrial herbicides or genetically modified organisms.

Biodynamic agriculture covers all aspects of agriculture: ecological, economic and social, including the use of biodynamic preparations, measures to organize the landscape, crop rotations, and the like.

As an example, the following is the composition of a biodynamic preparation used to **ENRICH THE EARTH**; it may seem more like a formula from a **medieval alchemy** primer or a **science fiction movie,** but its results are fiercely defended by those who use biodynamics:

Ground quartz is prepared and the horn of a cow is filled with it. The horn is buried in spring to be mined in autumn. One tablespoon of this quartz powder is mixed with 250 liters of water and sprayed on the vines under low pressure during the rainy season in order to prevent diseases caused by fungi.

FROM *TERROIR* TO BOTTLE

The vineyard is located in the Côte de Beaune, near the town of Beaune, in the region of Burgundy.

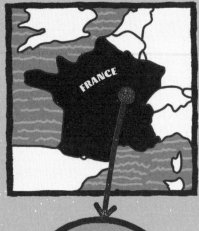

FRANCE

BOURGOGNE

Côte de Beaune

The parents of Chardonnay

Pinot Noir

Gouais Blanc

CHARDONNAY

(*It is common for a red wine variety crossed with a white wine variety to give rise to a white wine.*)

Only one variety

100 %
CHARDONNAY

Montrachet
GRAND CRU

DOMAINE LEFLAIVE

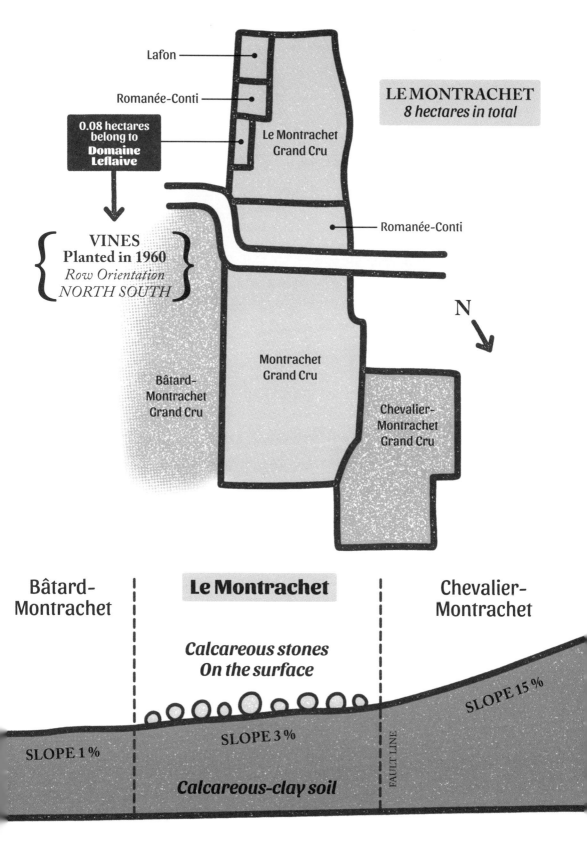

Lafon

Romanée-Conti

0.08 hectares belong to Domaine Leflaive

LE MONTRACHET
8 hectares in total

Le Montrachet Grand Cru

Romanée-Conti

{ **VINES**
Planted in 1960
Row Orientation
NORTH SOUTH }

N

Bâtard-Montrachet Grand Cru

Montrachet Grand Cru

Chevalier-Montrachet Grand Cru

Bâtard-Montrachet

Le Montrachet

Chevalier-Montrachet

Calcareous stones On the surface

SLOPE 15 %

SLOPE 3 %

SLOPE 1 %

FAULT LINE

Calcareous-clay soil

Hill of Grace

The Old World in Australia

The conquest of the promised land

> *"Sometimes you have to go through the wilderness before you get to the promised land."*
>
> <u>John Bytheway</u>

Perhaps they were divine signs.

Perhaps it was a true call from God.

For that reason, little by little, Johann Christian Henschke understood that it was time to leave the world he knew in search of the **promised land**. Because for a true Lutheran of Silesia like him, the religious decisions taken by the King of Prussia, <u>Frederick William III</u>, were intolerable. It was evident that the monarch's real purpose was to suppress the groups of **traditionalist Lutherans** to which the Henschke **FAMILY** belonged.

No, there was no other choice. They must leave forever....

On July 3, **1841**, Johann Christian, his wife, Appolonia Wilhelmine, and their three children embarked on the *Skjold* vessel bound for the Southern Hemisphere. This was a big opportunity. And maybe the last chance they would get.

Husbands and wives were to believe blindly in the signs God sent them. **"Australia"** was just a word to them, but that single word held the key to their future.

Johann Christian, having put his family in the hands of God, acted as if he were deeply convinced. He needed even more determination after the tragic death of Johanna Luise, their baby girl of 10 months, while they were waiting at the port.

Appolonia, devastated by the loss and surrounded by her three remaining children, boarded the ship with great anguish and uncertainty. **What fate would be revealed on the other side of the ocean?**

Tragically, **APPOLONIA WOULD NEVER REACH THAT PROMISED LAND.** During the voyage, she and her young son Johann Friedrich, age six, succumbed, like many others, to **dysentery.** As was customary in those cases, the bodies were thrown into the sea. Johann and his two sons were forced to face an unknown land alone. **THERE WOULD BE NO TURNING BACK.**

Johann Christian Henschke lost his wife and one of his sons during the boat journey. He arrived in Australia with only his two eldest sons.

Johann worked hard when he arrived in Australia, yet **his future and that of his children seemed increasingly uncertain**. Nevertheless, he remained diligent and was able to save some money. And after he ceased expecting anything of that promised land, he found <u>true promise and later salvation</u> in the splendid **EDEN VALLEY**, south of the continent.

Johan Christian Henschke would remarry in Australia, have eight more children and create perhaps the most prestigious vineyard in the country's history. It would be located at the foot of the small Lutheran church of Gnadenberg, in the vineyards known as Hill of Grace.

In 1868, together with his son Paul Gotthard, Johan Christian carried out the first harvest.

According to the very few documents that survived from that time, it was made up essentially of <u>Riesling</u> and <u>Shiraz</u>.

A few years later <u>Johann Christian</u> **died**, having fulfilled the dream of salvation for his family.

Paul Gotthard
Henschke

In 1873, <u>Paul Gotthard Henschke</u> took ownership of the property and planted more vineyards. Under his leadership, the production of the winery increased in quality and quantity. **Gotthard was also elected sheriff of the small community and was organist of the church of Gnadenberg, and he formed the Henschke family wind orchestra, with clarinets and horns that have been preserved until present day**.

The Henschke wines began to develop a true reputation.

In 1949, <u>Cyril Henschke</u>, a direct descendant of Johann Christian, studied the lands of the Valley of Eden and concluded that they were in fact ideal for producing **fine, dry, high-quality wines** and not the sweet wines that the winery had been making up to that point.

The current Henschke family: the couple, Stephen and Prue, and their children Andreas, Justine and Johann.

With the help of his brother Louis, Cyril made several modifications to the property and built a new fermentation cellar.

In 1958, he produced the first Henschke Hill of Grace, which marked the start of a true legend. For many it encapsulates the bravery, tireless work and desire of generations of immigrants who arrived in South Australia with the conviction that they should become masters of their future.

Since the death of Cyril in 1979, his son <u>Stephen</u> and <u>Stephen's wife</u>, Prue, have continued the family legacy and become **pioneers of organic** farming and biodynamics in Australia.

Since the 1980s, **A MULTITUDE OF CORPORATIONS HAVE ACQUIRED MANY OF THE REGION'S** family vineyards. But none has been able to buy Henschke.

"I became an expert at being able to say 'Go to hell' in many languages."

Stephen Henschke

"I became an expert at being able to say 'Go to hell' in many languages," says Stephen, who today has already put the fate of the vineyard in the hands of his children.

"Why would you sell a property with so much history and such a strong legacy? In addition, after six generations, we feel we are like the curators of a great museum." It was, after all, six generations ago that Johann Christian embarked for an unknown world for the salvation of his family and the generations to come.

"This history and this vineyard are a way of life for our family. And it's a very beautiful way to live one's life," says Stephen Henschke.

*Bio*dynamic generation

"Since I started using the principles
of biodynamics, I'm seeing the benefits
in a greater expression of aromas and textures
in the wines of all our vineyards."

Prue Henschke

The oldest parcels of the vineyard, dating back to 1860 and planted **without vine posts**, are known as the **Grandfather Block** and are some of the <u>oldest vines in the world</u>.

The <u>altitude</u> of the vineyard is **400 meters** above sea level.

The soils are <u>alluvial</u> and the earth is reddish thanks to a high <u>iron</u> content. The vineyard is subject to a **LARGE TEMPERATURE RANGE** between **day** and **night**.

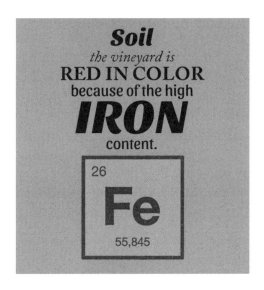

Soil
the vineyard is
RED IN COLOR
because of the high
IRON
content.

26
Fe
55,845

TODAY,
Stephen *(producer)*
and his wife,
Prune *(viticulturist)*
make up the
fifth generation
of the family, in charge of
the property together with the
sixth generation
of Henschkes:
their three children
**Justine, Johann
and Andreas.**

The price
of a bottle of
HENSCHKE
HILL OF GRACE
varies between
$400 *and* **$700.**

The vineyard uses
*organic and
biodynamic*
TECHNIQUES
for cultivation.

FROM *TERROIR* TO BOTTLE

The vineyard is located in the Valley of Eden, which is in the upper part of Borossa in Southern Australia.

AUSTRALIA

SOUTH AUSTRALIA

Keyneton

Hill of Grace
Grace is a translation of the German **Gnadenberg**.

The church in the Eden Valley is 150 years old.

Only one variety

100 % SHIRAZ

PLUMS

CHOCOLATE

BLACKBERRIES

Why shiraz and not syrah?

They are the same variety of French origin. Syrah is the best-known red wine variety in the Rhône region of France. The Australians simply decided to change its name.

The famous twisted 150-year-old vines in the **Grandfather Block.**

Photo: Lisa Perrotti Brown

BIODYNAMIC CULTIVATION

(*native pastures between rows*)

ALLUVIAL ORIGIN RED IRON-RICH SOILS ← - - - - **Area of the vineyard:** 4,55 ha

(altitude 400–500 masl)

Assemblage of 6 blocks or parcels, all very different thanks to their soils.

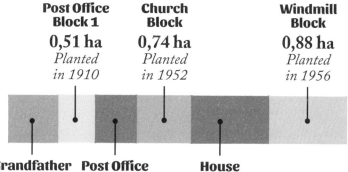

Post Office Block 1
0,51 ha
Planted in 1910

Church Block
0,74 ha
Planted in 1952

Windmill Block
0,88 ha
Planted in 1956

Grandfather Block
0,69 ha
Planted in 1860

Post Office Block 2
0,57 ha
Planted in 1965

House Block
1,08 ha
Planted in 1951

★ BARBARESCO, PIEMONTE ★

GAJA

Sorì San Lorenzo

The Holy Grail of Piedmont

The most collected Italian wine

"A great deal of happiness is given to men who are born where good wines are grown."

Leonardo da Vinci

Medieval legends tell that the Holy Grail —the cup that Jesus used to drink wine at the **Last Supper**— was delivered to **SAN LORENZO THE MARTYR** to be protected in a safe and secret place in the third century of the **CHRISTIAN ERA**.

Throughout the history of mankind, the Holy Grail has become a symbol of every sacred and occult object that could shelter supernatural powers and unimaginable revelations.

Perhaps, metaphorically, only grapes and wine can contain similar powers to the grail.

The coat of arms of Piemonte, the home of the Gaja family, which came originally from Spain.

That is why it is a revealing coincidence that a wine from Piemonte bears the name of "San Lorenzo," patron of the Holy Grail, because he is also the patron of **the Cathedral of Alba**, near the vineyards that Angelo Gaja would acquire in 1964.

Three centuries earlier, Gaja's ancestors had traveled through Spain, hiked the Pyrenees and crossed over to France until they reached Piemonte, on the other side of the Alps.

In 1859, after settling in Barbaresco for many years, Giovanni Gaja, aged 27, founded the winery that would change the history of Italian wine.

"Cabernet Sauvignon is to John Wayne what Nebbiolo is to Marcello Mastroianni."

Angelo Gaja

The Gaja family owned a tavern called Vapore ("steam"). It would only be a matter of time before they began to produce and sell their own wine at Cantina Vapore to accompany the traditional Italian dishes. In the beginning, the family only sold their wine to diners and neighbors. But soon, the Gajas began to market their wine throughout the area, gradually creating a following from customers who clamored to drink the Gaja wines year-round at their homes.

When the Gajas decided to sell the tavern, in 1912, they already had a wine following in the region, and this became one of the keys to their success.

In 1937 the name Gaja appeared on labels for the first time, in large red letters. And so the legend began.

A few years later, Angelo Gaja was born, the **leader** who would revolutionize the region and take his family winery well beyond the small town of Alba.

According to Angelo, he owes everything to his grandmother, Clotilde Rey. Clotilde was responsible for establishing both the winery's high quality standards and a hard work ethic, which she instilled in the young Angelo Gaja.

First came the canteen "Vapore"; then came the wine production.

> According to Angelo Gaja, **"An artisan** is one who learns from within **his own family**. I went to the school **of my father**, and that school was made up **of the cellar and the vineyards."**

Today Gaja winery ferments its wines in the **TRADITIONAL WAY,** for up to 30 days, as opposed to the **modern** fermentations of 5 days. *The entire process ends in* oak barrels from Slovenia that are up to **120 years old.**

"IT ALLOWS ME TO IMAGINE **the taste of a cross between Romanée-Conti and Mouton Rothschild",** SAYS ROBERT PARKER, JR., *the world's most celebrated wine critic, in reference to* **Gaja's Sorì San Lorenzo.**

GAIA GAJA, Angelo Gaja's daughter, **is the face of Gaja winery** worldwide. She works alongside **her siblings** Rosanna and Giovanni.

Painting of San Lorenzo from the 14th century, by the Italian painter Spinello Aretino.

Angelo says that his grandfather once told him: "In life, it can happen for a man to have a woman better than him. What to do? He has only two options. To follow her, or to kill her." "My grandfather was smart," says Angelo, "he asked his wife to help him run the business."

Clotilde had been born to a humble mountain family, in a village a few miles from the French border, and had studied to fulfill her dream of becoming a schoolteacher. In spite of this desire, **she soon began to take care of the winery's accounting, investments and correspondence**, and her efforts would allow the family to expand the business. When Clotilde died in 1961, her family's cellar had already become the most important in all of Barbaresco.

Angelo graduated from the school of viticulture and enology at Alba the year of his grandmother's death, in 1961. He furthered his studies in Montpellier and entered the University of Turin to study economics.

"Elegance does not need perfection."

Angelo Gaja

Like any revolutionary, Angelo **often fought with his father**, who felt protective of the wine-growing **traditions** of Piemonte.

The greatest conflict arose when Angelo decided to plant <u>Cabernet Sauvignon in Barbaresco</u>. He named it **"DARMAGI"** ("what a shame"), because those were the words his father said to Angelo when he first heard about the project. In the end, Angelo's father was right, because it would be the native **NEBBIOLO**, in the Costa Russi, Sorì Tildìn (named after grandmother Clotilde) and, of course, the Sorì San Lorenzo —the most memorable of all his vineyards— that would bring fame to the Gaja family and the region of Barbaresco.

It was there, beneath the earth, in the hidden roots of those vines, that Angelo found his Holy Grail.

"There is a religious nuance in the attitude towards the Nebbiolo in these lands. I know producers who spend their Sunday looking after their vineyards instead of going to Mass," says Federico Curtaz, Winery Manager and Angelo Gaja's right hand. "Maybe this is their way of worshiping God."

Angelo Gaja in his vineyards

FROM *TERROR* TO BOTTLE

The vineyard is located in Barbaresco, near the city of Alba, in the region of Piemonte, Italy.

ITALY

PIEMONTE

Barbaresco

A single variety
(since 2013, with Barbaresco denomination)

100 % NEBBIOLO

GAJA

SORI SAN LORENZO
1999

LANGHE

The first mention of the Nebbiolo grape variety is in the 13th century.

"Nebbiolo" is derived from the word nebbia ("fog" in English), a climatic phenomenon very common in Piedmont.

Because Nebbiolo needs a plentiful sun to ripen, it is planted on slopes.

Nebbiolo has high acidity and substantial tannins. And that is why a Gaja Sorì San Lorenzo can age and evolve favorably for many decades.

In 2016, Gaia Gaja, daughter of Angelo, and her siblings Rosanna and Giovanni decided to return to the Barbaresco denomination with their single vineyard wines, including Sorì San Lorenzo, which will be made with 100% Nebbiolo. This means that from the 2013 harvest onwards, the Gaja Sorì San Lorenzo will be made purely from Nebbiolo grapes.

The varieties of the blend
(1996–2013, named Langhe)

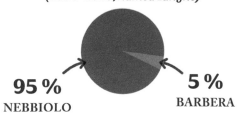

95 %
NEBBIOLO

5 %
BARBERA

At the end of the 1990s Angelo Gaja decided to stop using the Barbaresco denomination on his wines from the vineyards of Barbaresco —Sorì San Lorenzo, Sorì Tildin and Costa Russi— because in order to use the denomination, the wines would have had to be made entirely from Nebbiolo. Angelo objected to this restriction; he wanted to add, as his father and grandfather had, a touch (4–5%) of the variety Barbera, which had been banned in Barbaresco wines since the 1960s.

Sorì
means **"hillside with southern exposure"** in the Piemontese dialect.

San Lorenzo
is the name of the **Holy Guardian** of the city of Alba.

The Capital of Italian truffles

SOILS:
mixture of sand, silt and clay

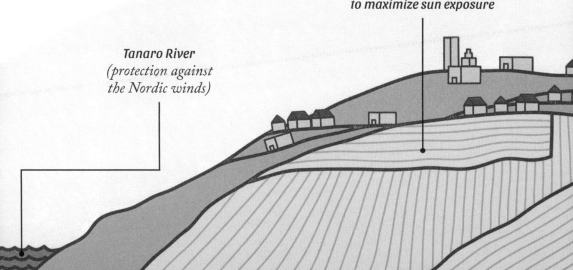

Vineyards on the hillside to maximize sun exposure

Tanaro River (protection against the Nordic winds)

CÔTE-RÔTIE, VALLÉE DU RHÔNE

E. GUIGAL

La Mouline

Red and white make magic

The soul
of the land of
the Rhône

*"A soul should be measured
by the dimension of its desire."*
<u>Gustave Flaubert</u>

Where does the story of a great wine begin?

When do the hundreds of elements —the alchemy of sun and time, earth and wind— combine to create that inexplicable magic of taste and longing?

What is really the starting point of an adventure of this magnitude?

World War I is over, and the **RHÔNE VALLEY,** a land of vineyards since Roman times, is slowly returning to its previous glory. There is famine all across Europe, and **many of the hillside vineyards** of the Côte Rôtie in the Northern Rhône **have been abandoned** or replaced by easier-to-farm fruit orchards. <u>A young boy</u> and his family settle in the region, and the boy soon becomes inseparable from his **BICYCLE**, spending his days transporting goods from one hillside to the next. One afternoon, when the entire valley is draped in brilliant sun-dappled light, the young man arrives on his bicycle to a small village. He stops, hops off his bike and is fascinated by what lies before him: the steep slope of the Côte-Rôtie, marked by an endless superposition of vines and ancient stone terraces. His name is **ETIENNE GUIGAL**, and on that day, he adds a new chapter to his collection of **dreams**: the vision of making wine and planting his own vineyard.

It is possible that the genesis of that miraculous Rhône Valley terrain occurred many millions of years earlier during the **COLOSSAL COLLISION** between two mountain ranges, the Massif Central and the Alps. This cataclysm changed the **shape of the European continent**, and also allowed the penetration of an enormous amount of water from the Mediterranean Sea to cover the South of France.

More recently, just 300 million years ago, volcanic activity deposited granite stones in the northern part of the Rhône. In the south, a huge amount of calcareous sediments formed the mountain chain known as the Dentelles de Montmirail.

Here, in this chain of mountains, the vertiginous 60-degree slope of the terraces ensures an intense exposure to the rays of the Mediterranean sun. Because of this particularity, locals say that these terraces are **"roasted"** in the sun. That is the meaning of **"Côte-Rôtie."**

The vine roots explore the depths of the earth to find, among other minerals, iron oxide. The <u>wind</u> blows and dries the grapes, protecting them from rot. Growing vineyards is difficult on those steep slopes, but the **payoff** is monumental.

We will never know the name of the man who came with the Romans to settle here. But in that valley, the Syrah variety had long been waiting for him.

Tsars, kings and nobles began to seek out the wines of the Rhône, and popes followed shortly afterward, both in Rome and in Avignon.

The **archives of Vidal-Fleury**, the oldest known wine entrepreneur in the region, testify to this history. The archives still contain the purchase orders of many famous wine buyers, including **Thomas Jefferson**, ambassador to France and future president of the United States.

> **"For more than 26 years I have been visiting vineyards and meeting their owners. And nowhere in the world have I found a producer as fanatic about quality as Marcel Guigal."**
>
> *Robert Parker, Jr.*

It was not long before the <u>legend</u> of the Rhône Valley and its vineyards began to come together with the story of a nobleman, Monsieur de Maugirón, who had two daughters, one **blond** and one **brunette**. The first daughter, the blond, would be awarded the vineyards of "La Côte Blonde," on the south side of the valley. Calcareous and rich in silica, these vineyards produce smooth and elegant wines. The brunette would be awarded the vineyards of the northern section, "La Côte Brune," well supplied with iron oxide and clay, to form the powerful flavor of highly age-worthy wines.

Guigal's La Mouline is born in the south, on the Côte Blonde.

Etienne Guigal and his son Marcel, with the Château d'Ampuis in the background.

Today, everyone in the Côte-Rôtie knows the name Guigal. The teenager who fell in love with the region's sun-dappled hillsides from atop his bike, and **labored hard** in the vineyards for 20 years, **BOUGHT** his own land in 1946 and created a legend. At first, many in the valley considered him a madman for his efforts to **transform the entire process of production and marketing** of wines and vineyards. He built small routes to distribute bottles through the valley, and stored wine in oak barrels for 42 months, longer than anyone else, among his many innovations.

Soon, his son Marcel joined the revolution, this time with an even more transcendental contribution than his palate: his eyes, because Etienne, his father, would become blind in 1961.

Father and son became a powerful force in the valley, who led not only their winery, but also their region, towards an infinitely superior scale of quality.

In a few years, the Guigals gained an <u>international reputation</u>. They builit a real **ROMAN VILLA** on their property, with an atrium, fountains, statues and stunning gardens.

In the mid-1980s, the Guigals bought the ancient property of Vidal-Fleury, where Etienne, as an adolescent, had taken his first steps in the world of wine.

In 1995, they would acquire the famous **Château d'Ampuis**, with its vineyards overlooking the Rhône.

In 2001 they would buy in Hermitage, Saint-Joseph and Crozes-Hermitage. They purchased the Domaine de Bonserine in 2006. And the list of **properties** keeps on growing.

This story has no end, however, because even though it spans millions of years, it is somehow still close to its birth. **Even today the dream of the land of the Rhône hides immense secrets.**

The Guigal family
BEGINS ITS WINEMAKING HISTORY
in 1946, *and in less than half a century*
becomes the dominant <u>property</u>
of the **Rhône Valley.**
THIS IS VERY RARE
IN THE FRENCH WINE WORLD,
where family traditions are generally **centuries old**
and in some cases even **millenarian.**

The vineyard La Mouline
is planted on
a steep *slope* and
in the form of a *semi-circle,*
thus resembling

a Roman
amphitheater.

E.GUIGAL

THE **3**
FAMOUS WINES
FROM GUIGAL ARE
La Turque,
La Mouline &
La Landonne.
They are known as
the three La La's.

THE GUIGAL FAMILY,
with Marcel and Philippe
leading the way,
build their
own barrels
to ensure that
EVERY DETAIL
OF THE PRODUCTION
of their wines is carried out
exactly as they like it.

E. GUIGAL

The name "Côte Rotie" means "roasted hillside" and refers to the sun exposure on the steep slopes, which gives intense aromas to the wines produced there.

FROM *TERROIR* TO BOTTLE

The vineyard is located in the Côte Blonde of the Côte Rotie, in the Rhône region, France.

FRANCE

RHÔNE-ALPS
● Côte Rôtie

89 % ➘ ➘ **11 %**
SYRAH   VIOGNIER

The **Viognier** white grape is co-fermented with the **red Syrah** and gives it aromatic complexity and softness. It is said that La Mouline is a feminine wine for this reason.

(*The wine is aged for 4 years in new French oak. La Mouline is so aromatic and concentrated that even after being in a new barrel for a full 4 years, the oak is barely perceptible.*)

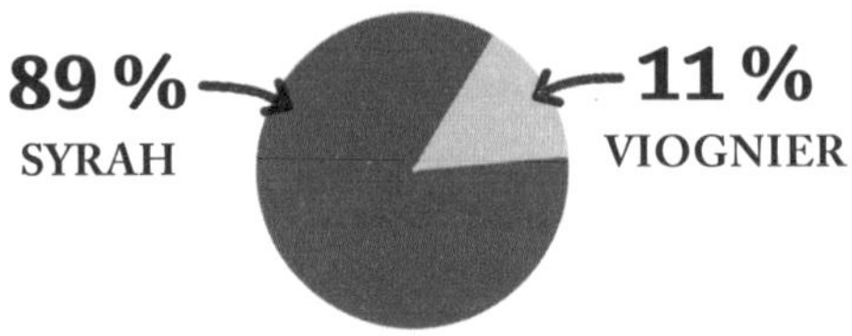

In the form of a Roman amphitheater

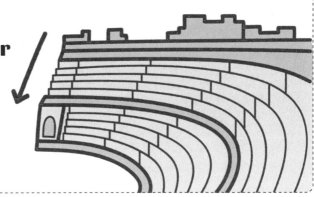

EXTREMELY STEEP

The oldest vineyard in the Côte-Rôtie

Some of the walls are more than **2400 years old**

1.5 hectares owned by Guigal **since 1966**

{ **Average age of the vines:** *70 years (some vines date back to 1890)* }

SOILS: gneiss and granite with areas of calcareous loess

★ GUALTALLARY, MENDOZA ★

CATENA ZAPATA

Adrianna Vineyard

The *Grand Cru* of South America

Adrianna's name was inspired by the readings of our mother Elena while she was pregnant: the story of the art and culture-loving Roman Emperor Hadrian, written by Marguerite Yourcenar.

The name also celebrates the Adriatic Sea, from which our great-grandfather Nicola Catena had sailed for the New World at the young age of 18, with a great dream as luggage.

The magic of altitude

*"To build is to collaborate with the land,
it is to leave a mark and humanize a landscape
which will be changed forever."*
<u>*Memoirs of Hadrian*</u>, Marguerite Yourcenar

Nicolás Catena Zapata grew up in the small rural town of La Libertad, where he worked in the vineyards **with his father and grandfather**. Nicolás studied at the local school where his mother **ANGÉLICA ZAPATA** was the headmaster. Nicolás' dream was to study physics in the United States. His mother, who imagined him dedicated to an <u>intellectual life</u>, shared that yearning with him. They both aspired to an unlikely destination for a young boy from the Argentine countryside: the dream of winning a **NOBEL PRIZE**.

At the age of only 18, a tragic accident robbed Nicolás of his mother Angélica and his grandfather Nicola, and of his dream for an academic life abroad. Feeling <u>responsible</u> for helping his father, who had fallen into an abyss of pain, Nicolás decided to stay in Argentina. Nicolás graduated as a **doctor in economics** in record time, and then took the reins of Catena Zapata, the family winery, at the age of 22.

In 2012, my father Nicolás Catena Zapata, his destiny marked by loss, was crowned with the last in a series of awards that would mark him as the most celebrated winemaker in the **Southern Hemisphere**.

In a Los Angeles salon he was awarded the Distinguished Service Award by *Wine Spectator* magazine (ironically, the likely equivalent to a Nobel in wine). In his acceptance speech, my father emphasized that all his achievements were due to the ***terroir of Mendoza***, to that land of opportunity to which my great-grandfather, his grandfather Nicola Catena, had arrived in 1902.

Although in our family we make a cult of work and study, my father believes in **luck** above all things. When I think of the way we came across the **ADRIANNA VINEYARD**, high up in the mountains, remote and seemingly hostile to the cultivation of the vine, I tend to agree with him.

Nicolás Catena Zapata had been led to believe that great wines only came from France. But after hearing about the epic win of Californian wines over French classics in the Judgment of Paris in the early 1980s, he asked himself: Why not strive to make a *GRAND CRU* IN ARGENTINA?

For the son of Angélica Zapata, the challenge was irresistible, and in his longing, Nicolás spent 10 intense years studying the terroir of Mendoza —particularly the high-altitude mountain climate and the **Malbec** grape— and traveled the world to learn from the best producers and vineyards. In Bordeaux, he met a Frenchman who told him, after sampling a Cabernet Sauvignon from a traditional area of Mendoza, that it <u>reminded him of a wine from a warm region</u>, and that it would have no aging potential.

That painful moment did nothing but inspire Nicolás, who threw himself towards the mountains, the mighty Andes, in search of the extreme limits of vine cultivation. Some 1,500 meters (almost 5,000 feet) up in elevation, Nicolás found **a place so cold and arid** that his own viticulturalist warned him that a vine would never ripen there. Today, on this site, lies the Adrianna Vineyard.

I cannot imagine a better name to represent the luck **OUR FAMILY** has had in finding its gold. My younger sister, Adrianna, accompanied our father in those early years of uncertainty when he dreamed of creating a *South American Grand Cru*.

Adrianna's name was inspired by the readings of our mother Elena while she was pregnant: the story of the art and culture-loving Roman **Emperor Hadrian**, written by Marguerite Yourcenar. The name also celebrates the **Adriatic Sea**, from which our great-grandfather Nicola Catena had sailed for the New World at the young age of 18, with a great dream as luggage.

From the beginning, the Adrianna vineyard yielded grapes and wines of the highest quality, but the capricious slope, the risk of frost, and the poor soils, calcareous and stony, made it very difficult to cultivate.

One day, standing at the top of the **PRIETO HILL** (baptized in honor of the manager who planted it, Don Prieto), I made the comment to the agronomist who accompanied me that the vines appeared uneven throughout the vineyard. He answered without hesitation that we should remove the plants with a bulldozer, mix up the soil and replant.

Nicola Catena
ate a lightly grilled rare
steak for breakfast every
morning to remind himself
of how lucky he had been to
reach the land of abundance
and opportunity that was
Argentina.

"Words do not do justice to this beauty."

Luis Gutiérrez, about the Adrianna Vineyard

After getting over the initial rage provoked by the vineyard manager's words, I realized that the great vineyards I had visited in Burgundy were characterized by their diversity **of soils and slopes**. I began to study with devotion each row of the Adrianna Vineyard, and not only each row, but every plant, every stone and every detail of the climate and soil.

I found that Adrianna lay on a <u>dry river</u> bed that over the years had transformed itself through volcanic, seismic and eolic activity to create **numerous plots**, each one rich in its diversity. When we vinified the grapes of each small plot of land separately, that was when we found the gold —the gold that no one expected to find on that barren, **REMOTE LAND**, which had been blessed by luck and destiny.

In the middle of the Adrianna Vineyard there is a unique plot, distinctive because of its **microbial richness**. Abundant rhizobacteria and mycorrhiza help the plants absorb nutrients and become perfectly adapted to their home. That is why we call the wine that comes from this parcel Mundus Bacillus Terrae or "Elegant Microbes of the Earth." These plants are a <u>pre-phylloxeric selection</u> drawn from our family's **Angélica vineyard**, which is already more than 90 years old.

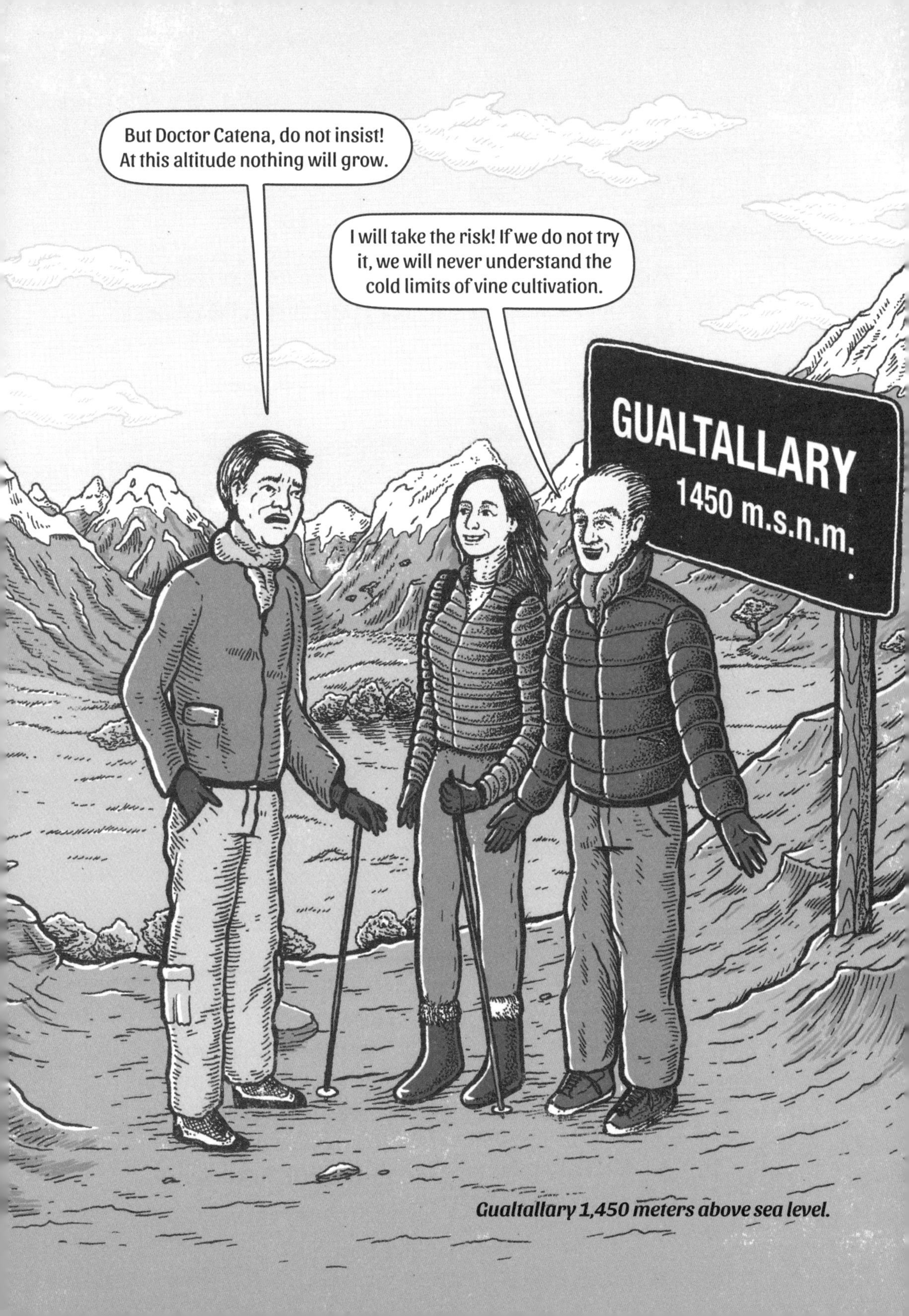

Gualtallary 1,450 meters above sea level.

100 POINT WINES from
Adrianna Vineyard

ADRIANNA VINEYARD
RIVER STONES
VINO DE PARCELA
MALBEC
2016

100

Robert Parker
WINE ADVOCATE
100pts

ADRIANNA VINEYARD
RIVER STONES
VINO DE PARCELA
MALBEC
2017

100

JAMES SUCKLING
100pts

ADRIANNA VINEYARD
FORTUNA TERRAE
VINO DE PARCELA
MALBEC
2017

100

JAMES SUCKLING
100pts

ADRIANNA VINEYARD
MUNDUS BACILLUS TERRAE
VINO DE PARCELA
MALBEC

100

falstaff
100pts

ADRIANNA VINEYARD
WHITE BONES
VINO DE PARCELA
CHARDONNAY
2018

100

JAMES SUCKLING
100pts

ADRIANNA VINEYARD
RIVER STONES
VINO DE PARCELA
MALBEC
2018

100

JAMES SUCKLING
100pts

In 1995
the Catena Institute of Wine
makes the first selection of
Argentine Malbec
from 80 year old vines.

CATENA ZAPATA
was named the
World's Most Admired Wine Brand 2020
by Drinks International.

IN 1999,
NICOLÁS
CATENA ZAPATA
formed a partnership with
DOMAINES BARONS DE ROTHSCHILD (LAFITE)
They decided to name the wine

CARO,
"CA", for **Catena**, and
"RO", for **Rothschild**.

Nicolás Catena Zapata
won the
"Decanter Man of the Year Award" in 2009,
and Distinguished
Service Awards from
Wine Spectator,
Der Feinschmecker
and **Wine Enthusiast**.

It is said that Malbec dates back to the times of the **Roman Empire** more than **2,000 years ago.**

MALBEC WAS FAMOUS IN **the Middle Ages,** where legend has it that **ELEANOR OF AQUITAINE** drank it in her **Court of Love.**

THE HISTORY OF ARGENTINE MALBEC

In 1855, at the time of the *Bordeaux Classification,* **the Grand Cru classés wines** *were composed of* **10-40 % malbec.**

In **1852** MALBEC IS CULTIVATED FOR THE FIRST TIME IN ARGENTINA, *where it becomes known as* **"The French Grape."**

Malbec is a delicate variety, harvested late and **VERY SUSCEPTIBLE TO COLD AND RAIN.** *That is why it adapts so well to the* **dry and sunny climate** of Mendoza.

After the **PHYLLOXERA EPIDEMIC of the late 19th century** which <u>devastated</u> Europe's vineyards, *Malbec practically* **disappeared from France.** *It was largely replaced by* **Cabernet Sauvignon and Merlot in Bordeaux.**

In 1990 Malbec underwent its renaissance in Argentina BEGINNING WITH THE WINES OF Nicolás Catena Zapata.

The Catena Institute of Wine **made the first** *massale* **and clonal selection** of Argentine Malbec *in 1995.* This selection of **135 PLANTS** IS IN ALL OF THE CATENA ZAPATA FAMILY VINEYARDS.

FROM *TERROIR* TO BOTTLE

The vineyard is located in Gualtallary, in the Uco Valley, in the province of Mendoza, Argentina.

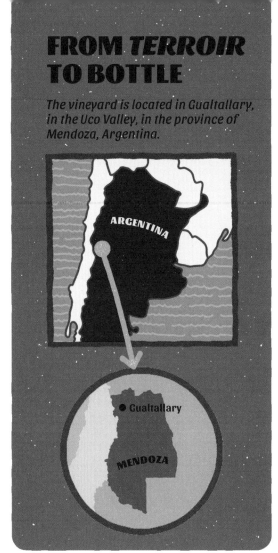

ARGENTINA

● Gualtallary

MENDOZA

The winery has a pyramidal shape to honor Argentina's Andean location, home to the highest vineyards in the world. The architecture was inspired by the Americas' Mayan civilization that aspired, like Catena Zapata, to reach the highest level in science, art and culture.

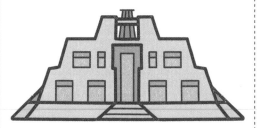

Only one variety

100 %
MALBEC

ADRIANNA VINEYARD
MUNDUS BACILLUS TERRAE
VINO DE PARCELA
MALBEC
2016
CATENA ZAPATA

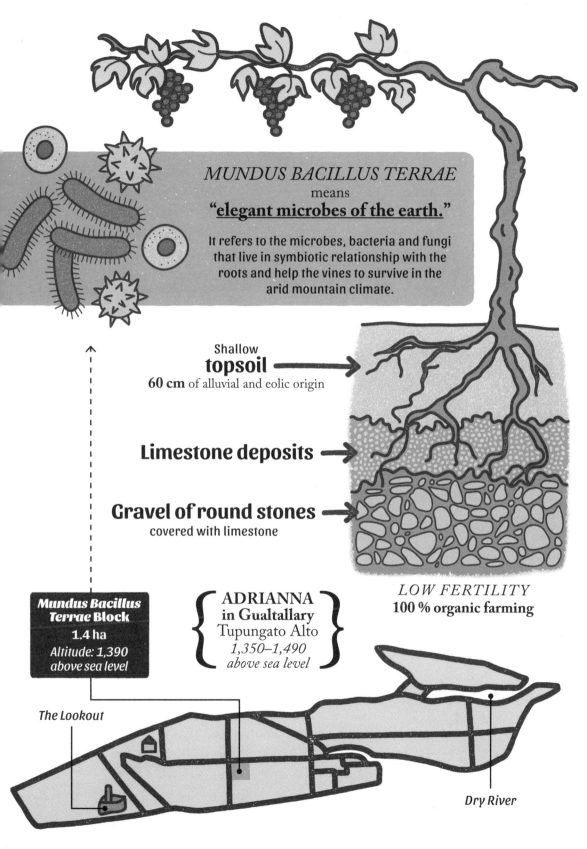

MUNDUS BACILLUS TERRAE
means
"elegant microbes of the earth."

It refers to the microbes, bacteria and fungi that live in symbiotic relationship with the roots and help the vines to survive in the arid mountain climate.

Shallow
topsoil
60 cm of alluvial and eolic origin

Limestone deposits

Gravel of round stones
covered with limestone

LOW FERTILITY
100 % organic farming

Mundus Bacillus Terrae Block
1.4 ha
Altitude: 1,390 above sea level

{ ADRIANNA
in Gualtallary
Tupungato Alto
1,350–1,490 above sea level }

The Lookout

Dry River

Laura Catena's
★ BIOGRAPHY ★

Dr. Laura Catena appeared in Oprah magazine as one of the World's
Top Women Vintners. Her work has been featured in the New York
Times, the Wall Street Journal, Food & Wine Magazine, La Nación,
Decanter and the Economist 1843 magazine, in an article about the
Catena Institute called "Argentine Wines' Premier Crew."

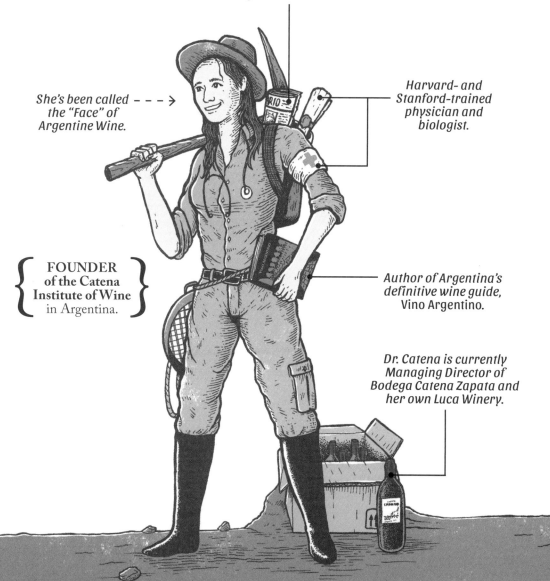

*She's been called - - - →
the "Face" of
Argentine Wine.*

*Harvard- and
Stanford-trained
physician and
biologist.*

{ **FOUNDER**
of the Catena
Institute of Wine
in Argentina. }

*Author of Argentina's
definitive wine guide,
Vino Argentino.*

*Dr. Catena is currently
Managing Director of
Bodega Catena Zapata and
her own Luca Winery.*

Gold in the vineyards
Laura Catena

editores

Avenida Donado 4694 - C1430DTP
Buenos Aires, Argentina
info@catapulta.net
www.catapulta.net

Idea & Authorship: Laura Catena

General editing: Victoria Blanco
Assistant editor: Agostina Martínez Márquez
Writing and research collaboration: Juan Pablo Domenech
Cover design, interior and infographics: Pablo Ayala
Cover illustrations and interior: Fernando Adorneti (Caveman)

First edition. Second reprint.

ISBN 978-987-637-666-2

Printed in China on May 2020.

Catena, Laura
   Gold in the vineyards / Laura Catena. - 1a ed . 2a reimp. - Ciudad
Autónoma de Buenos Aires : Catapulta , 2020.
   184 p. ; 22 x 17 cm.

   ISBN 978-987-637-666-2

   1. Vino. 2. Bodega. I. Título.
CDD 663.2

Credits:
P. 31: The Yorck Project: 10,000 Meisterwerke der Malerei. DVD-ROM, 2002. ISBN 3936122202.
Distributed by DIRECTMEDIA Publishing GmbH.
P. 41: Bibliothèque nationale de France
P. 47: Bureau of Engraving and Printing: U.S. Department of the Treasury
P. 51: John Yesberg
P. 70: This image is available from the United States Library of Congress's Prints and Photographs
division under the digital ID cph.3c23257
P. 76: http://www.usmint.gov/about_the_mint/coinLibrary/#sb1549
P. 84: en.wikipedia.org/wiki/Web_Gallery_of_Art P. 84: vintagegraphics.ohsonifty.com
P. 93: Wikipedia User: Wilson44691 / Mark A. Wilson
P. 97: thegraphicsfairy.com
P. 107: Weingut J.J. Prüm
P.125: vintagegraphics.ohsonifty.com
P. 137: Lisa Perrotti Brown
P. 145: Author: Spinello Aretino
P. 174: thegraphicsfairy.com